The London Coffee Guide.

2014

Edited by
Jeffrey Young
and Guy Simpson

Author: Allegra Strategies
Photography: Kate Beard, Maximilian Gower,
Joan Torrelles and Warattaya S. Bullôt
Design: John Osborne
Website: Tim Spring and Lee Goldsmith
Publisher: Allegra Publications Ltd

Allegra
PUBLICATIONS

Visit our website:
www.londoncoffeeguide.com

🐦 **@ldncoffeeguide**

All information was accurate at time of going to press.

Published by *Allegra* PUBLICATIONS Ltd © 2014

Walkden House, 10 Melton Street, London, NW1 2EB

Foreword

by **Anette Moldvaer**, Owner and Director of Coffee, Square Mile Coffee Roasters

When I first arrived in London ten years ago, I could count on one hand the number of cafés and roasteries that I could go to for a decent coffee. Coming from a barista background and working with some of the best coffees in the world, the gap between what I knew was possible, and what I found, was enormous. Outside of a small number of invested individuals, there seemed to be a lack of excitement or incentive to improve. There was little sense of community or open exchange within the industry, nor a unified drive to get a message of quality and care across to consumers. The opportunity for improvement seemed endless, and I made it my business to make a difference.

In the last five years, London has come on leaps and bounds. Numerous cafés have sprung up, and new roasteries have followed. Passionate coffee professionals and appreciative consumers have come out of the woodwork to talk coffee, enjoy coffee, and change coffee. With the boom we have had it would be easy to get complacent and lose momentum, but our coffee, service and barista skills need to keep developing for us to stay ahead of the game. Plenty of people have jumped onto the speciality coffee 'bandwagon' without the skills and knowledge to back it up. I have a lot of faith in the consumer to recognise and choose the best, most honest product, as long as we present it to them without boring or annoying them.

Unless the top tier of coffee keeps raising its game, our message will get lost in the noise of style over substance.

There is a lot more work to do, and we have room for a lot more good coffee, especially outside of Central and East London, not to mention the rest of the UK. Within the coffee community a network and a message has taken form, and while there is still room to refine and improve, the groundwork has been laid.

Contents

Introduction

Welcome to The London Coffee Guide 2014 – the definitive guide to London's independent coffee venues.

The Guide was born out of a desire to find the best and most interesting places to go for coffee in London. Following a boom in new openings since the first edition of the Guide in 2011, London is now home to a thriving, world-class independent coffee scene. The 2014 edition profiles 150 venues, an increase on the 130 featured last year, reflecting this exciting growth.

This book aims to assist and inform people who are keen to explore this vibrant city in a quest for fantastic coffee venues. We all visit cafés for different reasons: for many, coffee itself is the main attraction, for some, it's the buzz of visiting a unique coffee shop. Others go for the opportunity to relax, socialise or conduct business. Whatever your motivation, our objective is to encourage you to try something different and discover places you otherwise might never have known.

In this edition we have expanded the Coffee Knowledge chapter with two additional articles on the subjects of coffee grinding, and the importance of water in coffee brewing. We would like to thank all the industry experts for contributing their knowledge to help readers learn more about and experiment with the coffee they love.

Allegra is an established leader in consumer and business intelligence for the coffee industry in the UK and Europe. We have drawn on this research as well as experts in the field to compile this edition. We hope you enjoy it.

About the Guide

Ratings

Every venue featured in The London Coffee Guide 2014 has been visited and rated by our expert team. The ratings fall into two distinct categories: Coffee Rating and Overall Rating on a score of 1-5, with 5 being the highest possible score. Customer feedback received via The London Coffee Guide website and app also informs the venue shortlist and the final scores.

| COFFEE 4.75 / 5 | OVERALL 4.25 / 5 |

Coffee Rating

The Coffee Rating is about much more than just taste in the cup. An excellent coffee experience depends on a host of factors including: barista skills, coffee supplier, equipment, consistency, working processes and coffee presentation. The venue's coffee philosophy and commitment to excellence are also taken into consideration.

Overall Rating

In combination with the Coffee Rating, the Overall Rating reflects the total coffee shop experience for the customer. Factors taken into account include: service, café ambience, venue scale and impact, design and food quality. Feedback from the industry is also taken into consideration.

The Guide includes coffee carts and kiosks, as well as coffee shops. It was not considered fair to compare these venues with permanent cafés, so these venues have not been rated. The best carts, stalls and kiosks are grouped together in a separate chapter.

Key to symbols

Roaster		Toilets	
Alternative brew methods available		Parent & baby friendly	
Coffee beans sold on site		Disabled access	
Gluten-free products available		Wifi available	
Venue has a loyalty card		Licensed	
Soya milk available		Coffee courses available	
		Outdoor seating	

Venues marked as **NEW** are new to this edition of the Guide.

A Brief History of London Coffee Shops

THE EARLY YEARS

800 AD The coffee plant (Coffea) attracts human interest and consumption as early as 800 AD in the Kaffe region of Ethiopia. According to legend, it was an Ethiopian goat herder named Kaldi who first discovered how animated his herd of goats became after chewing on the red berries.

MID 17TH CENTURY

Travellers to Middle Eastern areas such as the Ottoman Empire bring coffee to Europe and Britain.

1650 The first English coffee house is established in Oxford by a Jewish gentleman named Jacob at the Angel in the parish of St Peter.

Coffee houses become meeting places for political and literary debates between artists, intellectuals, merchants and bankers. Such venues are known as Penny Universities, in reference to the one penny entrance fee. They are closely associated with reading and provide pamphlets and newspapers, as well as copious amounts of coffee.

1652 London's first coffee house is established by Pasqua Rosée in St Michael's Alley, Cornhill, London EC3.

1668 Edward Lloyd's Coffee House in Lombard Street becomes a key meeting place for ship owners and marine insurance brokers. Situated on the site occupied by Lloyds bank today, this coffee house likely contributed to London becoming a global hub for insurance and financial services.

1674 The Women's Petition Against Coffee is set up in London in response to men spending less time at home due to the "excessive use of the drying and enfeebling liquor".

1675 There are now more than 3,000 coffee houses across England. King Charles II attempts to outlaw coffee houses as hotbeds of revolution, but following large public protests, his proclamation is revoked after 11 days.

1680 Jonathan's Coffee House is established by Jonathan Miles in Change Alley. It is a place where stockbrokers frequently meet and eventually becomes today's London Stock Exchange.

1706 Thomas Twining opens the first known tea room in London, which can still be found at 216 Strand.

18TH CENTURY

Coffee houses gradually decline in popularity and become more elite establishments, when they start charging more than one penny for entrance. Travelling taverns replace coffee houses as popular social spaces. Coffee also becomes a less important commodity as the East India Company and British trade in general focuses more on tea imports from India.

LAST CENTURY

1894 Lyons opens a chain of tea rooms followed by Lyons Corner Houses in London's West End in 1906.

1923 The Kenya Coffee Company Limited (Kenco) is established and soon begins selling coffee on Vere Street, Mayfair.

1950s Italian-run espresso houses featuring Formica-topped tables are a popular feature of this era, particularly in London's Soho.

1952 Moka Bar opens on Frith Street and is London's first espresso bar.

1971 Starbucks opens its first store at Pike Place Market in Seattle, USA.

First Costa Coffee shop opened by brothers Sergio and Bruno Costa at 9 Newport Street, London.

1978 An early pioneer of artisanal coffee, Monmouth Coffee Company opens in Monmouth Street, Covent Garden.

1986 Pret A Manger is established by college friends Julian Metcalf and Sinclair Beecham.

1992 Fairtrade Foundation is established in London by the Catholic Overseas Development Agency, Christian Aid, Oxfam, Traidcraft, the World Development Movement, and the National Federation of Women's Institutes.

1995 Whitbread Group acquires Costa Coffee with 41 stores and a roastery in Lambeth.

1997 Nescafé opens first Café Nescafé trial stores in London and UK, but closes all outlets several years later.

Gerry Ford acquires five Caffè Nero stores and begins building a chain, which grows to become the third-largest coffee shop brand in the UK.

1998 Starbucks launches in the UK, acquiring 65 Seattle Coffee Company stores for an estimated £52 million.

1999 Allegra Strategies releases the groundbreaking Project Café Report, which predicts a significant boom in coffee shops.

LAST DECADE

2000 Internet cafés grow in popularity during the dotcom era.

Marks & Spencer launches Café Revive concept.

2001 The caffè latte is added to the Consumer Price Index (CPI), the basket of goods the government uses to measure products purchased by a typical British household.

2005 Flat White coffee shop opens in Berwick Street, Soho, setting the stage for further Antipodean influences on coffee in the UK.

2006 The number of branded chain coffee shop outlets exceeds 1,000 in London alone.

2007 James Hoffmann is crowned World Barista Champion and founds Square Mile Coffee Roasters.

2008 The first-ever European Coffee Symposium is held at London's Park Lane Hotel.

2009 A host of new artisanal "third wave" coffee shops open in London.

The UK's Gwilym Davies is crowned World Barista Champion.

2010 Costa, Starbucks and several other mainstream coffee chains launch their versions of the flat white.

The World Barista Championships are held in London at Caffè Culture.

The first edition of The London Coffee Guide is published.

2011 Growth of artisanal coffee shops and micro coffee roasteries in London continues to accelerate with the arrival of Workshop (formerly St. Ali), and Prufrock Coffee.

First-ever London Coffee Festival held at the Old Truman Brewery on Brick Lane.

2012 Roastery/cafés increase in popularity with the opening of Caravan King's Cross, Ozone and TAP Wardour Street.

London Coffee Festival hosts UK Barista Championship finals.

Harris + Hoole opens first London store.

2013 The London Coffee Festival is attended by over 16,000 visitors.

Bulldog Edition opens at Ace Hotel London, in collaboration with Square Mile Coffee Roasters.

West End

London's West End is synonymous with the city's legendary theatre and music scene, as well as its restaurants, shopping and nightlife. Business people and actors rub shoulders with tourists and urbanites, and the area's café culture is just as diverse.

* NEW
◊ TOP 30

The Attendant

27a Foley Street, W1W 6DY

The Attendant is a coffee bar sited in a former Victorian public lavatory. This astonishing conversion has artfully preserved several original features. Suffice to say that the cups and saucers are not the only porcelain the visitor will encounter. Caravan coffee is accompanied by a mouth-watering array of New York deli style sandwiches, which can be ordered through the toilet attendant's old window. Don't be shy to spend a penny or two at one of London's most original coffee venues.

+44(0)20 7637 3794
www.the-attendant.com
⊖ Goodge Street / Oxford Circus

MON-FRI. 8:00am - 6:00pm
SAT. 9:00am - 6:00pm
SUN. 9:00am - 4:00pm

First opened 2013
Roaster Caravan
Machine La Marzocco GB/5, 2 groups
Grinder Mazzer Robur E

Espresso £2.20
Cappuccino £2.80
Latte £2.80
Flat white £2.80

MAP REF. **1**

COFFEE 4.50 / 5	OVERALL 4.25 / 5

The Borough Barista

60 Seymour Street, W1H 7JN

Borough Barista provides an artisanal alternative to the high street chains that predominate in West London. This venue provides a calm oasis of blonde wood and friendly service just around the corner from Marble Arch. The large downstairs seating area provides ample space for a business meeting, or to spread out with the Saturday papers. The chocolaty 'St James' espresso blend is custom roasted for Borough Barista, and enjoyed in crisp surroundings by a smart Mayfair crowd.

+44(0)20 7563 7222
www.theboroughbarista.com
⊖ Marble Arch

MON-FRI. 8:00am - 5:00pm
SAT. 9:00am - 5:00pm
SUN. Closed

First opened 2011
Roaster Union Hand-Roasted custom blend
Machine La Marzocco Linea, 2 groups
Grinder Mazzer Super Jolly, Eureka

Espresso £1.80 / £2.00
Cappuccino £2.60 / £3.00
Latte £2.60 / £3.00
Flat white £2.60 / £3.00

MAP REF. **2**

COFFEE 4.00 / 5	OVERALL 4.25 / 5

DunneFrankowski at Sharps

9 Windmill Street, W1T 2JF

NEW

An impressive collaboration with Sharps Barbers is the latest endeavour by well-groomed coffee gents Rob Dunne and Victor Frankowski. The space is smartly partitioned: barber shop and coffee bar complementing one other without a whisker of encroachment. Coffee here is top drawer, featuring guest beans from renowned international roasters. There's an intriguing food offer too, including a series of pop-up lunchtime food residences by independent food companies. The café feels very neatly pulled together as a whole; every detail from the trim tiling to clean-cut branding befits this dapper Fitzrovia location.

www.dunnefrankowski.com
⊖ Goodge Street

MON-FRI. 8:00am - 6:00pm
SAT. 10:00am - 6:00pm
SUN. 12:00am - 6:00pm

First opened 2013
Roaster Various UK and international roasters
Machine Kees van der Westen Spirit, 3 groups
Grinder Mahlkönig K30, Mahlkönig EK 43

Espresso £2.00
Cappuccino £2.40
Latte £2.40
Flat white £2.40

MAP REF. ❸

COFFEE 4.75 / 5   **OVERALL** 4.50 / 5 ★★★★½

Fernandez & Wells Somerset House

Somerset House, Strand, WC2R 1LA

This prestigious venue occupies three rooms in one of London's most beautiful buildings. Customers are treated to the very best of everything: Sicilian panettone, Amalfi lemons, the finest meats, cheeses and European wines...the list goes on. At the beating heart of the operation is a Synesso Cyncra, handled by a skilled team of baristas who also prepare delicate single estate filter coffees. This is more than a café - it is a fine food and coffee emporium.

+44(0)20 7420 9408
www.fernandezandwells.com
⊖ Temple

Sister locations Beak Street / Lexington Street / South Kensington

MON-FRI. 8:00am - 10:00pm
SAT. 10:00am - 10:00pm
SUN. 10:00am - 8:00pm

First opened 2011
Roaster Has Bean bespoke blend
Machine Synesso Cyncra, 3 groups
Grinder Mazzer Robur E x2,
Mahlkönig Tanzania

Espresso £2.40
Cappuccino £2.80
Latte £2.80
Flat white £2.80

MAP REF. **4**

COFFEE 4.50 / 5	OVERALL 4.50 / 5

Kaffeine

66 Great Titchfield Street, W1W 7QJ

Since opening in 2009, Kaffeine has established itself as one of London's pre-eminent coffee venues. Australian owner Peter Dore-Smith sets the bar high and his team strives to provide the best experience possible for all, from casual lunch customers to coffee experts. This café is distinguished by its impeccable attention to detail, from the stylish wooden interior to the food made fresh on site, and the precise latte art poured on each carefully crafted coffee. Kaffeine has developed a loyal following and remains a source of inspiration for London's coffee community.

+44(0)20 7580 6755
www.kaffeine.co.uk
⊖ Oxford Circus

MON-FRI. 7:30am - 6:00pm
SAT. 8:30am - 6:00pm
SUN. 9:00am - 5:00pm

First opened 2009
Roaster Square Mile Coffee Roasters
Machine Synesso Cyncra, 3 groups
Grinder Mazzer Robur E, Anfim

Espresso £1.90 / £2.40
Cappuccino £2.80
Latte £2.80
Flat white £2.70

MAP REF. **5**

COFFEE 4.75 / 5	OVERALL 5 / 5
🫘🫘🫘🫘🫘	★★★★★

Lantana

13 Charlotte Place, W1T 1SN

Stylish and understated Fitzrovia favourite Lantana has gone from strength to strength since opening in 2008. This café and eatery is always abuzz with chatter and filled with loyal patrons, particularly during the weekend when its legendary brunch menu has customers queuing out the door. The coffee here is of a consistently high quality, both on the main premises and at the second shopfront next door that caters just for takeaway traffic.

+44(0)20 7637 3347
www.lantanacafe.co.uk
⊖ Goodge Street / Tottenham Court Road

Sister locations Salvation Jane

MON–FRI. 8:00am – 6:00pm
SAT–SUN. 9:00am – 5:00pm

First opened 2008
Roaster Square Mile Coffee Roasters
Machine La Marzocco Linea, 3 groups
Grinder Mazzer Robur E, Anfim

Espresso £2.00
Cappuccino £2.60
Latte £2.60
Flat white £2.60

MAP REF. **6**

COFFEE 4.50 / 5   OVERALL 4.50 / 5 ★★★★½

8

Monmouth Coffee Company Covent Gdn

27 Monmouth Street, WC2H 9EU

This is where the Monmouth phenomenon began, back in 1978. The original Monmouth roastery occupied this site until 2007 when it moved to Bermondsey. The interior here is simple, focusing attention on the coffee. Wooden booths encourage strangers to share conversation and trade ideas, continuing the grand tradition of the capital's first coffee houses. Monmouth Coffee is nothing short of a London institution, and more often than not, queues snake out of the door, but it's definitely worth the wait.

+44(0)20 7232 3010
www.monmouthcoffee.co.uk
⊖ Covent Garden

Sister locations Borough / Bermondsey

MON–SAT. 8:00am – 6:30pm
SUN. Closed

First opened 1978
Roaster Monmouth Coffee Company
Machine La Marzocco Linea, 3 groups
Grinder Mazzer Robur E

Espresso £1.50
Cappuccino £2.50
Latte £2.50
Flat white £2.50

MAP REF. **7**

COFFEE 4.50 / 5   **OVERALL** 4.50 / 5   ★★★★⯪

Monocle Café

18 Chiltern Street, W1U 7QA

West End

Monocle Café is an impeccably curated coffee shop belonging to Tyler Brûlé's global current affairs, business and lifestyle magazine.
The café bears all the hallmarks of Monocle's slick aspirational brand and design-conscious outlook. Every item is meticulously sourced, from the midcentury-style furniture, right down to the teaspoons and barista aprons.
A small kitchen downstairs serves up plates of elegant fare, but it's the Swedish cinnamon buns and Japanese cakes that really steal the show.

+44(0)20 7135 2040
www.cafe.monocle.com
🚇 Baker Street

MON-FRI. 7:00am - 7:00pm
SAT. 9:00am - 6:00pm
SUN. 10:00am - 6:00pm

First opened 2013
Roaster Allpress Espresso
Machine La Marzocco Linea, 2 groups
Grinder Mazzer Robur, Mazzer Super Jolly

Espresso £2.50
Cappuccino £3.00
Latte £3.00
Flat white £3.00

MAP REF. **8**

COFFEE 4.00 / 5   OVERALL 4.25 / 5 ★★★★½

10

New Row Coffee

24 New Row, WC2N 4LA

This miniature coffee house is staffed by super friendly coffee obsessives who discuss latte art in their downtime and prepare the best flat white on a street crammed with other outlets. Daily filter options are available at the bar, along with an enticing lemon drizzle cake, gourmet cookies and a range of pastries and sandwiches. Fresh almond milk is prepared each day, and the pulp is used to make tasty almond biscuits.

+44(0)20 3583 6949
www.newrowcoffee.co.uk
⊖ Leicester Square / Charing Cross

Sister locations FreeState Coffee

MON-THU. 7:30am - 7:00pm
FRI. 7:30am - 8:00pm
SAT. 9:00am - 8:00pm
SUN. 9:00am - 6:00pm

First opened 2011
Roaster Union Hand-Roasted and guests
Machine La Marzocco Linea, 3 groups
Grinder Mazzer Major, Mazzer Super Jolly

Espresso £2.00
Cappuccino £2.60
Latte £2.60
Flat white £2.50

MAP REF. **9**

COFFEE 4.25 / 5   OVERALL 4.00 / 5   ★★★★☆

Notes Covent Garden

TOP 30

36 Wellington Street, WC2E 7BD

Situated close to the Royal Opera House, this café is the perfect place for lovers of the arts to browse racks of music and films. In 2013 Notes established its own roasting operation, delivering impressive espresso blends and single estate beans. Participating in the 'One Farmer, One Roaster' project, the company works directly with individual Ethiopian coffee farmers to help improve their farm infrastructure. Notes is much more than just a coffee bar; it also runs tasting evenings for coffee and wine, and holds regular live jazz evenings.

+44(0)20 7240 7899
www.notes-uk.co.uk
⊖ Covent Garden

Sister locations Trafalgar Square

MON-WED. 8:00am - 9:00pm
THU-FRI. 8:00am - 10:00pm
SAT. 9:00am - 10:00pm
SUN. 10:00am - 6:00pm

First opened 2011
Roaster Notes Roastery
Machine La Marzocco Strada, 3 groups
Grinder Mazzer Robur E, Anfim, Mahlkönig Tanzania

Espresso £2.20 / £2.40
Cappuccino £2.80
Latte £2.80
Flat white £2.80

MAP REF. **10**

COFFEE 4.75 / 5   OVERALL 4.50 / 5   ★★★★½

Notes Trafalgar Square

31 St Martin's Lane, WC2N 4ER

Notes Trafalgar Square was the first venue opened by Brazilian coffee entrepreneur Fabio Ferreira. Occupying a stunning room with high ceilings, large mirrors and a refined yet welcoming atmosphere, this is a coffee house that looks to London's past for its decor but is distinctly forward-looking in its coffee philosophy. The progressive coffee menu is complemented by a range of fine foods. In the evening, the café transforms into a wine bar, and theatre-goers in the know drop by to sample the range of excellent wines, spirits, cheeses and charcuterie.

+44(0)20 7240 0424
www.notes-uk.co.uk
⊖ Charing Cross / Leicester Square

Sister locations Covent Garden

MON-WED. 7:30am - 9:00pm
THU-FRI. 7:30am - 10:00pm
SAT. 9:00am - 10:00pm
SUN. 10:00am - 6:00pm

First opened 2010
Roaster Notes Roastery
Machine La Marzocco Strada, 3 groups
Grinder Mazzer Robur, Anfim, Mahlkönig Tanzania

Espresso £2.20 / £2.40
Cappuccino £2.80
Latte £2.80
Flat white £2.80

MAP REF. **11**

COFFEE 4.75 / 5

OVERALL 4.50 / 5 ★★★★☆

The Providores and Tapa Room

109 Marylebone High Street, W1U 4RX

Run by New Zealand chef Peter Gordon, The Providores and Tapa Room is a fusion restaurant, café and wine bar with a distinct South Pacific flavour. The ground floor Tapa room features a huge Rarotongan tapa cloth on one wall and heaves with people at breakfast, while the dining room upstairs caters for a more formal lunch and dinner crowd. Coffee is supplied by up-and-coming roastery Volcano Coffee Works, the perfect accompaniment to a delicious brunch at this popular venue.

+44(0)20 7935 6175
www.theprovidores.co.uk
⊖ Baker Street / Bond Street

Sister locations Kopapa

MON-FRI. 8:30am - 11:00pm
SAT. 9:00am - 11:00pm
SUN. 9:00am - 10:30pm

First opened 2001
Roaster Volcano Coffee Works
Machine La Marzocco GB/5, 2 groups
Grinder Mazzer Super Jolly

Espresso £2.00 / £2.40
Cappuccino £2.80
Latte £2.80
Flat white £2.80

MAP REF. **12**

COFFEE 4.00 / 5   OVERALL 4.25 / 5

TAP Coffee Rathbone Place

26 Rathbone Place, W1T 1JD

TAP Coffee was one of the first London coffee bars to break with convention and offer a selection of different espresso blends.
The venue's design theme blends burnished wood and steel with attractive features such as a Belfast sink filled with chilled drinks, and the classic delivery bicycle parked at the door. The Rathbone Place store is a popular hangout for Fitzrovia admen, who mastermind advertising campaigns over perfectly-poured flat whites.

+44(0)20 7580 2163
www.tapcoffee.co.uk
⊖ Tottenham Court Road / Goodge Street

Sister locations Tottenham Court Road / Wardour Street

MON-FRI. 8:00am - 7:00pm
SAT. 10:00am - 6:00pm
SUN. Closed

First opened 2010
Roaster TAP Coffee
Machine Nuova Simonelli Aurelia II T3, 2 groups
Grinder Mazzer Robur E, Mazzer Kony E, Mazzer Super Jolly E, Mahlkönig Tanzania

Espresso £2.20
Cappuccino £2.60
Latte £2.60
Flat white £2.60

MAP REF. **13**

COFFEE 4.50 / 5	🫘 🫘 🫘 🫘 🫘	OVERALL 4.50 / 5	★ ★ ★ ★ ✦

TAP Coffee Tottenham Court Road

114 Tottenham Court Road, W1T 5AH

TAP's unbranded facade sets it apart on chain-dominated Tottenham Court Road. Look closer and you'll notice a vintage bicycle suspended above the doorway; a motif which also graces the takeaway cups and ingeniously illustrated loyalty cards.
The interior fuses exposed light bulbs, copper piping and white ceramic that recalls London's Victorian heyday. The attention to detail displayed towards the design is also evident in the coffee preparation. The baristas use separate blends for espresso and milk coffees, and single origin beans can be sampled on filter.

+44(0)20 7580 2163
www.tapcoffee.co.uk
⊖ Warren Street

Sister locations Rathbone Place / Wardour Street

MON–FRI. 8:00am - 7:00pm
SAT. 10:00am - 6:00pm
SUN. Closed

First opened 2011
Roaster TAP Coffee
Machine Nuova Simonelli Aurelia II T3, 2 groups
Grinder Mazzer Robur E, Mazzer Kony E, Mazzer Super Jolly E, Mahlkönig Tanzania

Espresso £2.20
Cappuccino £2.60
Latte £2.60
Flat white £2.60

MAP REF. **14**

COFFEE 4.50 / 5	🫘🫘🫘🫘🫘	OVERALL 4.50 / 5	★★★★⯪

Taylor St Baristas Mayfair

22 Brooks Mews, W1K 4DY

Hidden away down a little mews, this small café is popular with suited up professionals. The sunlit interior features dark antique furniture, a slate floor and reclaimed church pews. The Taylor St independent chain has built its reputation on consistently excellent coffee, but just as importantly, well-trained and friendly staff. This is especially true at the Mayfair store, where baristas and customers banter freely with one another, and has led to the creation of the competitive 'Super frequent coffee freaks' loyalty blackboard.

+44(0)20 7629 3163
www.taylor-st.com
⊖ Bond Street

Sister locations New Street / Shoreditch / Canary Wharf / Monument / Bank / South Quay

MON-FRI. 7:30am - 5:30pm
SAT-SUN. Closed

First opened 2011
Roaster Union Hand-Roasted and guests
Machine La Marzocco Linea, 3 groups
Grinder Mazzer Kony E, Mazzer Super Jolly, Anfim

Espresso £2.00
Cappuccino £3.00
Latte £3.00
Flat white £3.00 / £3.30

MAP REF. **15**

COFFEE 4.50 / 5   OVERALL 4.50 / 5

Timberyard Seven Dials

7 Upper St Martin's Lane, WC2H 9DL

Timberyard's second outpost replicates the winning formula of the original Clerkenwell store. Split over two floors, the comfortable seating area downstairs is perfect for working away on a laptop, and two dedicated rooms are available to hire for business meetings or other gatherings. Customers can try the excellent Has Bean coffee brewed by Chemex as well as espresso, and the stellar tea service also deserves a special mention. Each teapot is served with a timer to ensure optimal brew time.

www.timberyardlondon.com
⊖ Covent Garden

Sister locations Clerkenwell

MON-FRI. 8:00am - 8:00pm
SAT. 10:00am - 8:00pm
SUN. 10:00am - 6:00pm

First opened 2014
Roaster Has Bean
Machine La Marzzoco FB/80, 3 groups
Grinder Anfim, Mahlkönig Vario

Espresso £2.20
Cappuccino £2.80
Latte £2.80
Flat white £2.70

MAP REF. **16**

COFFEE 4.50 / 5	OVERALL 4.50 / 5

Workshop Coffee Co. Marylebone

75 Wigmore Street, W1U 1QD

At this smaller outpost of Workshop Coffee Co., espresso is a science and its baristas are laureates of the highest order. This is coffee at its best, brewed with clinical precision and minute attention to detail. This location provides the blueprint for a new kind of coffee bar, with a sleek marble and dark wood interior, simple bar-style seating, a small range of pastries enshrined behind polished glass and a range of Workshop beans and coffee-making equipment available to buy.

+44(0)20 7253 5754
www.workshopcoffee.com
◉ Bond Street

Sister locations Clerkenwell / Holborn

MON-FRI. 7:00am - 7:00pm
SAT-SUN. 9:00am - 6:00pm

First opened 2011
Roaster Workshop Coffee Co.
Machine Synesso Hydra, 3 groups
Grinder Mazzer Robur x2, Mazzer Major, Mahlkönig Tanzania

Espresso £2.00
Cappuccino £2.80
Latte £3.00
Flat white £2.80

MAP REF. **17**

COFFEE 4.75 / 5

OVERALL 4.50 / 5 ★★★★½

18

Helping baristas *innovate* for 30 years

Almond Fruit Smoothie

Almond Iced Coffee

Soya Cappuccino

Our voyage of discovery started over 30 years ago but we continue to ask ourselves what other everyday alternatives to milk could we make to give coffee bar lovers even more ways to enjoy plant power?

alpro *enjoy plant power*

feed your curiosity enjoy plant power

www.alpro.com/uk

Soho

Famous for its outrageous nightlife, Soho is also well-known for its cutting-edge bars, clubs and restaurants. This spirit of experimentation and adventure extends to coffee and many of London's most exciting artisanal cafés can be found here.

Fernandez & Wells Beak Street

73 Beak Street, W1F 9SR

This venue perfects Fernandez & Wells' signature combination of artisanal European food with superb coffee. Fernandez & Wells was one of the first coffee bars in London to install the high-end Synesso Cyncra espresso machine. This café retains its simple focus on fine coffee and food. The clean interior accentuates this priority with unadorned cream walls and rustic timber benches. Fernandez & Wells retains its position as a premier London coffee and foodie destination.

+44(0)20 7287 8124
www.fernandezandwells.com
⊖ Piccadilly Circus / Oxford Circus

Sister locations Lexington Street / South Kensington / Somerset House

MON-FRI. 7:30am - 6:00pm
SAT-SUN. 9:00am - 6:00pm

First opened 2007
Roaster Has Bean bespoke blend
Machine Synesso Cyncra, 3 groups
Grinder Mazzer Robur E, Ditting

Espresso £2.40
Cappuccino £2.80
Latte £2.80
Flat white £2.80

MAP REF. **18**

COFFEE 4.50 / 5   OVERALL 4.50 / 5   ★★★★☆

22

Flat White

17 Berwick Street, W1F 0PT

Established in 2005, Flat White was one of the first cafés to bring antipodean-style coffee to the UK. It has become a London coffee institution, celebrated as a pioneer of third wave coffee in the capital. The departure of original co-owner Cameron McClure and other staff resulted in a period of decline, but fortunately a new team is now in place with a renewed focus on quality. The interior has been refreshed and further exciting developments are planned. Customers can expect a bespoke single origin roast from Square Mile, pulled through an impressive 4-group Synesso, affectionately dubbed "The Orca".

+44(0)20 7734 0370
www.flatwhitecafe.com
⊖ Oxford Circus / Tottenham Court Road

Sister locations Milkbar

MON-FRI. 8:00am - 7:00pm
SAT-SUN. 9:00am - 6:00pm

First opened 2005
Roaster Square Mile Coffee Roasters bespoke roast
Machine Synesso Hydra, 4 groups
Grinder Mazzer Robur E, Mazzer Robur

Espresso £2.00
Cappuccino £2.50
Latte £2.50
Flat white £2.50

MAP REF. **19**

COFFEE 4.50 / 5

OVERALL 4.50 / 5 ★★★★⯪

Soho

Foxcroft & Ginger

3 Berwick Street, W1F 0DR

This modern-rustic Soho coffee house is a key feature of the vibrant Berwick Street community. A heavy wooden door leads into an industrial space decorated with a mixture of concrete, tile, brick and exposed piping. The intimate downstairs area offers a welcome retreat. In addition to hearty brunches and small wine menu, Foxcroft & Ginger bake their own sourdough bread and serve up delicious pizzas.

www.foxcroftandginger.co.uk
⊖ Piccadilly Circus / Oxford Circus

MON. 8:00am – 7:00pm
TUE-FRI. 8:00am – 10:00pm
SAT. 9:00am – 10:00pm
SUN. 9:00am – 7:00pm

First opened 2010
Roaster Caravan, Has Bean, The Roasting Party
Machine Synesso Cyncra, 3 groups
Grinder Anfim x2

Espresso £2.00
Cappuccino £2.50
Latte £2.50
Flat white £2.50

MAP REF. **20**

COFFEE 4.50 / 5	🫘🫘🫘🫘🫘	OVERALL 4.25 / 5	★★★★⯪

Milkbar

3 Bateman Street, W1D 4AG

(NEW)

Milkbar emerged from beneath the wing of Flat White to become one of Soho's most popular brunch venues. It has grown into a mecca for Kiwis and Aussies longing for a taste of home, and a place of discovery for Londoners experiencing Square Mile's daringly light roasts. After a year in transition, this much-loved antipodean café is returning to form with a fresh team and renewed enthusiasm. The baristas' disarming informality, together with the venue's youthful, grungy feel make it a popular hangout for Soho creatives.

+44(0)20 7287 4796
⊖ Tottenham Court Road / Leicester Square

Sister locations Flat White

MON-FRI. 8:00am – 10:00pm
SAT-SUN. 9:00am – 9:00pm

First opened 2008
Roaster Square Mile Coffee Roasters bespoke roast
Machine La Marzocco FB/80, 3 groups
Grinder Mazzer Robur, Mazzer Super Jolly, Ditting

Espresso £2.00
Cappuccino £2.50
Latte £2.50
Flat white £2.50

MAP REF. **21**

COFFEE 4.50 / 5	🫘🫘🫘🫘🫘	OVERALL 4.25 / 5	★★★★⯪

Nude Espresso Soho

19 Soho Square, W1D 3QN

Nude Espresso's signature East blend coffee has arrived in Soho. The interior here is sleeker and more understated than Nude Hanbury Street, but the staff are just as passionate about delivering excellent coffee to their urbane Soho customers. A range of tasty breakfast, lunch and sweet foods are prepared fresh by Nude chefs in the open kitchen. A selection of coffee equipment is also available to purchase, and Nude runs home brewing workshops to help customers get the most from their gear.

+44(0)7712 899 336
www.nudeespresso.com
⊖ Tottenham Court Road

Sister locations Hanbury Street / Nude Espresso Roastery

MON-FRI. 8:00am - 5:00pm
SAT-SUN. Closed

First opened 2011
Roaster Nude Coffee Roasters
Machine La Marzocco FB/80 3 groups
Grinder Compak K-10 Professional x3

Espresso £2.00
Cappuccino £2.60
Latte £2.60
Flat white £2.60

MAP REF. **22**

COFFEE 4.50 / 5 🫘🫘🫘🫘🫘 OVERALL 4.25 / 5 ★★★★☆

Princi

135 Wardour Street, W1F 0UT

A buzzing, lively eatery, Princi is a perfect fit for Soho and is packed with hungry customers all hours of the day and night. One length of the venue is occupied by tantalising displays of croissants, tarts, cakes, pizza and salads all made on site. The elegant dining area consists of granite tables and a long metal bench against a water-feature wall, and the large window frontage is perfect for people-watching on this entertaining street.

+44(0)20 7478 8888
www.princi.co.uk
⊖ Piccadilly Circus / Oxford Circus / Tottenham Court Road

MON-SAT. 8:00am - 12:00am
SUN. 8:30am - 10:00pm

First opened 2008
Roaster Small Batch Coffee Company
Machine Synesso Cyncra, 3 groups
Grinder Mazzer Robur

Espresso £1.60
Cappuccino £2.30
Latte £2.30
Flat white £2.40

MAP REF. **23**

COFFEE 3.75 / 5 🫘🫘🫘🫘◗ OVERALL 4.25 / 5 ★★★★☆

Soho

Rapha Cycle Club

85 Brewer Street, W1F 9ZN

The perfectionism Rapha applies to its cycling gear is readily apparent in its approach to coffee; the espresso here is extraordinarily good. Try a shot made with German JB Kaffee, pulled through a customised Synesso Hydra. Bike locks are available for those arriving on two wheels, and the vintage Italian cycling memorabilia makes a fascinating addition to the recently enlarged space. Coffee is no afterthought here; Rapha has established itself as a coffee destination in its own right.

+44(0)20 7494 9831
www.rapha.cc
⊖ Piccadilly Circus

MON–FRI. 7:30am – 9:00pm
SAT. 8:30am – 7:00pm
SUN. 10:00am – 6:00pm

First opened 2012
Roaster JB Kaffee, Workshop Coffee Co.
Machine Synesso Hydra, 2 groups
Grinder Anfim x2, Mahlkönig Tanzania

Espresso £2.00 / £2.50
Flat white £2.75 / £3.00

MAP REF. **24**

Sacred Ganton Street

13 Ganton Street, W1F 9BL

Soho

The Sacred empire now extends across five London locations but this is where it all began back in 2005. Owners Tubbs Wanigasekera and Matt Clark are proud New Zealanders and this shines through in the decor and relaxed atmosphere that characterises this busy café. While the main upstairs area has a pleasing openness that extends out into the bustle of Carnaby Street, couches in the mellow basement area offer a cosy refuge in which to sip a cup of the delicious New Zealand-style house roast.

+44(0)20 7734 1415
www.sacredcafe.com
⊖ Oxford Circus

Sister locations Covent Garden (Stanfords) / Highbury Studios / Westfield / Torrington Place

MON-FRI. 7:30am - 8:00pm
SAT-SUN. 10:00am - 7:00pm

First opened 2005
Roaster Sacred House Roast
Machine La Marzocco Linea, 3 groups
Grinder Anfim Super Caimano, Mazzer Super Jolly

Espresso £2.10
Cappuccino £2.90 / £3.10
Latte £2.90 / £3.10
Flat white £2.90 / £3.10

MAP REF. **25**

COFFEE 4.25 / 5	🫘 🫘 🫘 🫘 🫘	OVERALL 4.50 / 5	★ ★ ★ ★ ⯪

Speakeasy Espresso & Brew Bar

3 Lowndes Court, W1F 7HD

Occupying a light, modern space just off Carnaby Street, Speakeasy is home to some of London's most talented baristas. There's more to this stylish coffee bar than meets the eye. Speakeasy encourages a hands-on approach to coffee making, operating a coffee school in their dedicated downstairs space. In addition, free drop-in sessions are run on Thursdays 5-7pm, when budding home baristas can seek advice and get hands-on with a range of equipment from cold water drippers to a domestic Rocket espresso machine.

www.speakeasycoffee.co.uk
Oxford Circus

Sister locations Department of Coffee and Social Affairs / The Liberty of Norton Folgate / Chancery Coffee / Tonic Coffee Bar

MON-WED. 8:00am - 7:00pm
THU-FRI. 8:00am - 8:30pm
SAT. 10:00am - 8:30pm
SUN. 10:00am - 6:00pm

First opened 2011
Roaster Climpson & Sons bespoke blend
Machine La Marzocco FB/80, 3 groups
Grinder Mazzer Robur E x2, Mazzer Super Jolly, Mahlkönig Tanzania

Espresso £2.20
Cappuccino £2.70 / £2.90
Latte £2.70 / £2.90
Flat white £2.50

MAP REF. 26

COFFEE 4.50 / 5   OVERALL 4.50 / 5 ★★★★

TAP Coffee Wardour Street

193 Wardour Street, W1F 8ZF

Formerly known as Tapped & Packed, TAP Coffee's newest venue is an impressive statement in coffee bar design. Two rows of tables draw the eye towards the magnificent Probat roaster. Low-hung spotlights highlight the interior's bare wood and gleaming steel fixtures. TAP serves its excellent house-roasted 'Jack of Spades' blend, and single origins at the dedicated brew bar. Connoisseurs will also appreciate the green tea offered as a palate cleanser. Visitors can expect exceptionally high standards from one of London's most accomplished coffee destinations.

+44(0)20 7580 2163
www.tapcoffee.co.uk
⊖ Tottenham Court Road

Sister locations Rathbone Place / Tottenham Court Road

MON-FRI. 8:00am - 7:00pm
SAT. 10:00am - 6:00pm
SUN. 12:00pm - 6:00pm

First opened 2012
Roaster TAP Coffee
Machine Nuova Simonelli Aurelia T3, 3 groups
Grinder Mazzer Robur E, Mazzer Kony E, Mazzer Super Jolly E, Mahlkönig Tanzania

Espresso £2.20
Cappuccino £2.60
Latte £2.60
Flat white £2.60

MAP REF. **27**

COFFEE 4.75 / 5 🫘🫘🫘🫘🫘   **OVERALL** 4.75 / 5 ★★★★★

Tonic Coffee Bar

15 Sherwood Street, W1F 7ED

NEW

The latest venue from Coffeesmiths Collective is a modern and sophisticated take on the traditional Italian espresso bar. Tonic is ideal for picking up an expertly-made brew before dashing to your next Soho appointment, but owing to the small space, it's not the best place to spread out with the broadsheets. Alongside the consistently excellent Climpson & Sons espresso blend, coffee aficionados will delight in the rotating range of guest filter coffees brewed by Filtro Shuttle.

www.toniccoffeebar.co.uk
⊖ Piccadilly Circus

Sister locations Speakeasy Espresso & Brew Bar / Department of Coffee & Social Affairs / Chancery Coffee / The Liberty of Norton Folgate

MON-FRI. 7:30am - 5:30pm
SAT SUN. 9:30am - 5:30pm

First opened 2013
Roaster Climpson & Sons bespoke blend
Machine La Marzocco FB/80, 2 groups
Grinder Mazzer Robur E x2, Mazzer Super Jolly, Mahlkönig Vario

Espresso £2.20 / £2.30
Cappuccino £2.70 / £2.90
Latte £2.70 / £2.90
Flat white £2.50

MAP REF. 28

COFFEE 4.25 / 5   OVERALL 4.25 / 5   ★★★★☆

Holborn
& Bloomsbury

Dotted with beautiful squares and grand architecture, Bloomsbury offers refined, contemplative surroundings to enjoy coffee. Home to thinkers for centuries, the neighbourhood is anchored by numerous academic institutions and the imposing British Museum, as well as boasting a wealth of literary connections. Busy Holborn to the south is frequented by lawyers and journalists, conducting business in and around the many cafés.

Artigiano Holborn

104 New Oxford Street, WC1A 1HB

NEW

Artigiano brings a mix of artisanal coffee and produce to the notoriously touristy end of Oxford Street. The expansive dual-level location is a slick coffee haven by day, and transforms into a wine bar at night. Customers have the choice of Origin Coffee's espresso blend, or more unusual single estate espressos, served by well-trained baristas with some seriously high-end equipment. Establishing itself as a small independent chain, Artigiano is helping change expectations of coffee on the high street.

www.artigiano.uk.com
⊖ Tottenham Court Road

Sister locations St Paul's

MON-TUE. 7:30am - 9:30pm
WED-FRI. 7:30am - 10:30pm
SAT-SUN. 9:00am - 10:30pm

First opened 2013
Roaster Origin Coffee
Machine La Marzocco Strada, 3 groups x2
Grinder Mazzer Major x2

Espresso £1.75 / £2.25
Cappuccino £2.50 / £2.75
Latte £2.50 / £2.75
Flat white £2.50

MAP REF. **29**

COFFEE 4.25 / 5   OVERALL 4.50 / 5 ★★★★⯪

Bea's of Bloomsbury Bloomsbury

44 Theobald's Road, WC1X 8NW

The selection of baked goods on display at Bea's is enough to make any cake-lover go weak at the knees. The bakery café also claims to be the inventor of the delightfully named 'duffin', a doughnut and muffin hybrid. Customers can purchase a selection of cakes to go, or enjoy lunch or afternoon tea while watching the bakery's famous creations being made. The freshly prepared coffee provides the perfect accompaniment for any of Bea's decadent treats.

+44(0)20 7242 8330
www.beasofbloomsbury.com
⊖ Chancery Lane / Holborn

Sister locations One New Change

MON-FRI. 8:00am - 7:00pm
SAT-SUN. 12:00pm - 7:00pm

First opened 2008
Roaster The Drury Tea & Coffee Company
Machine La Marzocco Linea, 2 groups
Grinder Mazzer Super Jolly, Anfim

Espresso £1.70 / £2.00
Cappuccino £2.40 / £2.70
Latte £2.40 / £2.70
Flat white £2.40 / £2.70

MAP REF. **30**

COFFEE 3.75 / 5   OVERALL 4.00 / 5 ★★★★☆

Chancery Coffee

90 Chancery Lane, WC2A 1DT

Chancery Coffee's friendly baristas demonstrate meticulous attention to detail at the controls of their bright red La Marzocco FB/80. The magnificent copper counter forms the focal point in the small space. In an honourable nod to the professional associations of barristers, the café's branding incorporates the four emblematic creatures of the Inns of Court. The coffee is made to a consistently excellent standard, but with seating limited to a narrow bench, we suggest having yours to go.

www.chancerycoffee.co.uk
⊖ Chancery Lane

Sister locations Department of Coffee and Social Affairs / Speakeasy Espresso & Brew Bar / The Liberty of Norton Folgate / Tonic Coffee Bar

MON-FRI. 7:30am - 5:00pm
SAT-SUN. Closed

First opened 2012
Roaster Climpson & Sons bespoke blend
Machine La Marzocco FB/80, 3 groups
Grinder Mazzer Robur E, Mazzer Super Jolly E

Espresso £2.20
Cappuccino £2.70 / £2.80
Latte £2.70 / £2.80
Flat white £2.50

MAP REF. **31**

COFFEE 4.25 / 5   OVERALL 4.25 / 5 ★★★★☆

Continental Stores

54 Tavistock Place, WC1H 9RG

NEW

Continental Stores is a new venture from the owners of highly regarded Store Street Espresso. The lofty ceilings and white walls create an unhurried, contemplative environment in which to catch up on reading or meet friends. A mixed crowd of professionals, students and academics trade ideas and conversation against a backdrop of modern artworks. With plenty of experience behind them and an enviable equipment setup, the barista team ensure the Square Mile coffee is presented at its best.

Russell Square / King's Cross St Pancras

Sister locations Store Street Espresso

MON–FRI. 7:30am - 7:00pm
SAT. 9:00am - 5:00pm
SUN. Closed

First opened 2014
Roaster Square Mile Coffee Roasters and guests
Machine Synesso Cyncra, 3 groups
Grinder Nuova Simonelli Mythos, Mahlkönig EK 43

Espresso £1.80 / £2.00
Cappuccino £2.50
Latte £2.50
Flat white £2.50

MAP REF. **32**

COFFEE 4.50 / 5

OVERALL 4.50 / 5 ★★★★☆

The Espresso Room

31-35 Great Ormond Street, WC1N 3HZ

Despite The Espresso Room's pocket-sized proportions, the amiable baristas manage the queue with practiced ease, pulling shots on the Synesso Hydra with utmost precision. Owner Ben Townsend is a sage figure in the capital's coffee scene, and can also be found leading coffee courses at the London School of Coffee. This tiny espresso bar is widely considered one of London's very best, with a focus on coffee quality few others can match. Join the line of hospital staff, lawyers, and dapper Lamb's Conduit fashionistas to discover why.

+44(0)7760 714 883
www.theespressoroom.com
⊖ Russell Square

MON-FRI. 7:30am - 5:00pm
SAT-SUN. Closed

First opened 2009
Roaster Round Hill Roastery, Square Mile Coffee Roasters, JB Kaffee and others
Machine Synesso Hydra, 2 groups
Grinder Mazzer Robur E, Mahlkönig EK 43

Espresso £1.80 / £2.20
Cappuccino £2.80 / £3.40
Latte £2.80 / £3.40
Flat white £2.80 / £3.40

MAP REF. **33**

COFFEE 4.75 / 5 🫘 🫘 🫘 🫘 🫘   OVERALL 4.25 / 5 ★ ★ ★ ★ ☆

FreeState Coffee

23 Southampton Row, WC1B 5HA

Raising the banner for third wave coffee in Holborn, FreeState's experienced baristas serve excellent coffee with a dose of American-style enthusiasm. Mismatched furniture and an old school gym bench add character to the sunny interior. Opened by the team behind New Row Coffee, the café builds on its coffee pedigree with a wider selection of Union roasts and guest beans. Customers with time to linger can opt for single estate filter coffee served at the dedicated brew bar.

+44(0)20 7998 1017
www.freestatecoffee.co.uk
⊖ Holborn

Sister locations New Row Coffee

MON-FRI. 7:00am - 7:00pm
SAT-SUN. 9:00am - 6:00pm

First opened 2013
Roaster Union Hand-Roasted and guests
Machine La Marzocco Strada EP, 3 groups
Grinder Mazzer Robur E, Mazzer Super Jolly x3

Espresso £2.00
Cappuccino £2.60 / £3.40
Latte £2.60 / £3.40
Flat white £2.50

MAP REF. **34**

COFFEE 4.50 / 5   OVERALL 4.25 / 5 ★★★★☆

Store Street Espresso

This exciting venue joined the burgeoning foodie scene on Store Street in 2010 and crowds of hungry students and creatives have been flocking here ever since for the great coffee and electric atmosphere. The café itself is stylish and light-filled, with an ambience that encourages customers to linger for leisure, study or work. A passionate team of baristas serve Square Mile coffee on a Synesso Hydra, and regularly offer guest coffees from up-and-coming roasters such as Leeds' North Star.

⊖ Goodge Street

MON–FRI. 7:30am - 7:00pm
SAT. 9:00am - 6:00pm
SUN. 10:00am - 5:00pm

First opened 2010
Roaster Square Mile Coffee Roasters
Machine Synesso Hydra, 2 groups
Grinder Mazzer Robur E, Anfim

Espresso £1.80 / £2.00
Cappuccino £2.50
Latte £2.50
Flat white £2.50

MAP REF. **35**

| COFFEE 4.50 / 5 | 🫘 🫘 🫘 🫘 🫘 | OVERALL 4.50 / 5 | ★ ★ ★ ★ ✦ |

Farringdon & Clerkenwell

Formerly hubs of manufacturing and enterprise, the districts of Farringdon and Clerkenwell now house smart offices, loft apartments, night clubs and restaurants. Some of the most exciting coffee venues in town can also be found here, making this the new heart of London's burgeoning coffee culture.

Caravan Exmouth Market

11-13 Exmouth Market, EC1R 4QD

Photo: Gary Handley

Caravan roastery and restaurant is a popular fixture on the diverse Exmouth Market food and coffee scene. This modern dining venue is always busy, particularly on sunny days when patrons spill out onto the pavement.
Plenty of options on the menu make this a popular destination for a weekend brunch or casual dinner. As well as espresso, a wide variety of coffee brewing methods are on offer, allowing patrons to appreciate the full range of flavours found in Caravan house roasts.

+44(0)20 7833 8115
www.caravanonexmouth.co.uk
⊖ Angel / Farringdon

Sister locations King's Cross

MON-WED. 8:00am - 11:00pm
THU-FRI. 8:00am - 12:00am
SAT. 10:00am - 12:00am
SUN. 10:00am - 10:30pm

First opened 2010
Roaster Caravan Coffee Roasters
Machine La Marzocco FB/80, 3 groups
Grinder Mazzer Robur E x2, Ditting KR 804, Mahlkönig K30

Espresso £2.00
Cappuccino £2.60
Latte £2.60
Flat white £2.60

MAP REF. **36**

| COFFEE 4.50 / 5 | 🫘🫘🫘🫘🫘 | OVERALL 4.50 / 5 | ★★★★⯪ |

42

Department of Coffee and Social Affairs

14-16 Leather Lane, EC1N 7SU

Part of the The Coffeesmiths Collective, Department of Coffee and Social Affairs is a key player on the booming Farringdon coffee scene. Occupying a former ironmonger's premises across two shopfronts, this generous space features an unpolished wood and exposed brick theme with plentiful seating. A reclaimed copper boiler displayed on the counter makes for an intriguing focal point. The Climpson & Sons espresso, roasted in Hackney, is supplemented by alternating guest coffees from other roasters.

www.departmentofcoffee.co.uk
⊖ Chancery Lane / Farringdon

Sister locations Speakeasy Espresso & Brew Bar / The Liberty of Norton Folgate / Chancery Coffee / Tonic Coffee Bar

MON-FRI. 7:00am - 6:00pm
SAT-SUN. 10:00am - 4:00pm

First opened 2010
Roaster Climpson & Sons bespoke blend and others
Machine La Marzocco FB/80, 3 groups
Grinder Mazzer Robur E x2, Mazzer Super Jolly

Espresso £2.20
Cappuccino £2.70 / £2.90
Latte £2.70 / £2.90
Flat white £2.50

MAP REF. **37**

COFFEE **4.50 / 5** 🫘🫘🫘🫘🫘   OVERALL **4.25 / 5** ★★★★★

Farm Collective Farringdon

91 Cowcross Street, EC1M 6BH

Farm Collective takes pride in sourcing high-quality, fresh, ethical produce directly from British farms. This emphasis on quality extends to the excellent Square Mile coffee, best enjoyed together with a signature peanut butter brownie. Farm also offer Tregothnan teas, the only tea grown in England. The tantalising food display makes this a great destination for a quick drop-in. However, the small space and limited seating means it's often best to opt for takeaway at busy periods.

+44(0)20 7253 2142
www.farmcollective.com
⊖ Farringdon

Sister locations Bank / Gray's Inn Road

MON-FRI. 7:00am - 3:30pm
SAT-SUN. Closed

First opened 2009
Roaster Square Mile Coffee Roasters
Machine La Marzocco Linea, 2 groups
Grinder Anfim

Espresso £1.80 / £2.10
Cappuccino £2.30 / £2.60
Latte £2.30 / £2.60
Flat white £2.40 / £2.70

MAP REF. **38**

COFFEE 4.00 / 5	OVERALL 4.00 / 5

Fix

161 Whitecross Street, EC1Y 8JL

Discreetly occupying a former pub adjacent to the Whitecross St Market, Fix is a spacious and stylish place to drop in for a coffee and bite to eat. Fix serves a Climpson's blend custom-roasted to their exact specification. Big leather couches, well-chosen vintage furniture and quirky light fittings make this a comfortable and dynamic space in which to hang out. Creatives and visitors to the Whitecross Street market keep Fix buzzing on weekdays.

+44(0)20 7998 3878
www.fix-coffee.co.uk
⊖ Old Street / Barbican

Sister locations Fix 126

MON-FRI. 7:00am - 7:00pm
SAT. 8:00am - 7:00pm
SUN. 9:00am - 7:00pm

First opened 2009
Roaster Climpson & Sons bespoke blend
Machine La Marzocco Linea, 3 groups
Grinder Mazzer Robur E, Mazzer Super Jolly E

Espresso £1.50 / £1.80
Cappuccino £2.30 / £2.50
Latte £2.30 / £2.50
Flat white £2.30

MAP REF. **39**

COFFEE 4.25 / 5	OVERALL 4.25 / 5

Ground Control

61 Amwell Street, EC1R 1UR

The Ethiopian Coffee Company's mission is to showcase the very best coffees from this unique part of Africa, including Yirgacheffe, Harrar and Sidamo. The company's Clerkenwell café, Ground Control, combines traditional Ethiopian curios with the sharp, space-age lines of a Kees van der Westen Mirage coffee machine. The company also retails beans at the Real Food Market behind the Southbank Centre (Fridays-Sundays) and Partridges Specialist Food Market in Chelsea (Saturdays).

+44(0)20 7502 1201
www.theethiopiancoffeecompany.co.uk
⊖ Angel

MON. 7:30am - 4:00pm
TUE-FRI. 7:30am - 5:00pm
SAT. 8:00am - 5:00pm
SUN. 9:00am - 4:00pm

First opened 2012
Roaster The Ethiopian Coffee Company
Machine Kees van der Westen Mirage, 2 groups
Grinder Mazzer Super Jolly

Espresso £2.00
Cappuccino £2.50
Latte £2.50
Flat white £2.50

MAP REF. **40**

COFFEE 4.50 / 5	🫘🫘🫘🫘🫘	OVERALL 4.25 / 5	★★★★✫

Look Mum No Hands! Clerkenwell

TOP 30

49 Old Street, EC1V 9HX

Look Mum No Hands! has rapidly become one of the city's busiest destinations for those who love bikes and coffee in equal measure. This lively cafe and bike workshop is decorated with bicycles, bike parts, and vintage cycling memorabilia. The outdoor area is now home to a coffee stall (a former RAF aircraft repair cart no less), which dispenses coffee to cyclists and pedestrians in a rush. A new range of British craft beer is available, and during the Tour de France, this place is a full-on party zone. If you love bikes, coffee or both, Look Mum No Hands! is an essential destination.

+44(0)20 7253 1025
www.lookmumnohands.com
⊖ Old Street / Barbican

Sister locations Hackney

MON-FRI. 7:00am - 10:00pm
SAT. 9:00am - 10:00pm
SUN. 9:30am - 10:00pm

First opened 2010
Roaster Square Mile Coffee Roasters and guests
Machine Kees Van Der Westen Mirage, 2 groups, La Marzocco Linea, 2 groups
Grinder Anfim x3, Mazzer Super Jolly

Espresso £2.00
Cappuccino £2.80
Latte £2.80
Flat white £2.60

MAP REF. 41

COFFEE 4.50 / 5

OVERALL 4.50 / 5 ★★★★⯪

Prufrock Coffee

23-25 Leather Lane, EC1N 7TE

Photo: Micha Theiner

Farringdon & Clerkenwell

Prufrock has achieved cult status in London, and international recognition for its progressive methods and tireless pursuit of coffee excellence. Founded by Gwilym Davies (2009 World Barista Champion) and Jeremy Challender, Prufrock is a premier destination to see unusual brew methods and sample rare coffees. The space also incorporates the Barista Resource And Training school (BRAT). The extremely knowledgeable staff are enthusiastic about their craft, and welcoming to all.

+44(0)20 7242 0467
www.prufrockcoffee.com
Farringdon / Chancery Lane

MON-FRI. 8:00am - 6:00pm
SAT. 10:00am - 5:00pm
SUN. 10:00am - 5:00pm

First opened 2011
Roaster Square Mile Coffee Roasters and guests
Machine Nuova Simonelli Aurelia II T3, Victoria Arduino Athena Leva, 2 groups
Grinder Mahlkönig Tanzania, Mahlkönig K30, Nuova Simonelli Mythos

Espresso £2.20 / £2.60
Cappuccino £2.80 / £3.00
Latte £3.00
Flat white £2.80

MAP REF. **42**

COFFEE 5 / 5	OVERALL 4.75 / 5

Timberyard Clerkenwell

61-67 Old Street, EC1V 9HW

Neither rough-hewn nor rustic, as its name might suggest, Timberyard is a slick yet friendly operation with big ambitions. The large tables and comfy seating downstairs make the space perfect for work or business meetings. iPads pre-loaded with subscriptions to popular news sites are also available to use. Timberyard offers some excellent coffee options, including Has Bean's citrusy 'Jabberwocky' blend. Single estate coffees brewed by Chemex are ideal to share with a coffee-loving friend.

+44(0)20 3217 2009
www.timberyardlondon.com
⊖ Old Street / Barbican

Sister locations Seven Dials

MON-FRI. 8:00am - 8:00pm
SAT. 10:00am - 8:00pm
SUN. 10:00am - 6:00pm

First opened 2012
Roaster Has Bean
Machine La Marzocco FB/80, 3 groups
Grinder Anfim, Mahlkönig Vario, Mahlkönig Tanzania

Espresso £2.20
Cappuccino £2.80
Latte £2.80
Flat white £2.70

MAP REF. **43**

COFFEE 4.50 / 5

OVERALL 4.50 / 5

Workshop Coffee Co. Clerkenwell

27 Clerkenwell Road, EC1M 5RN

Formerly known as St Ali, Workshop Coffee has experienced a meteoric rise. This temple to speciality coffee contains a café, restaurant and roastery, spanning multiple floors of an industrial themed space. A remarkable 'living wall' of plants adds a dash of green to the raw brick and steel. Attracting top talent from the UK, Australia and the US, Workshop is a young company with a reputation for roasting excellence. An array or single origins and popular 'Cult of Done' espresso blend are crafted on-site, and their coffee is now a frequent sight in some of the capital's finest coffee bars.

+44(0)20 7253 5754
www.workshopcoffee.com
⊖ Farringdon

Sister locations Marylebone / Holborn

MON. 7:30am – 6:00pm
TUE-FRI. 7:30am – 10:00pm
SAT-SUN. 8:00am – 6:00pm

First opened 2011
Roaster Workshop Coffee Co.
Machine La Marzocco Linea PB, 3 groups, La Marzocco Linea, 2 groups
Grinder Mazzer Robur E x3, Mazzer Major E, Mahlkönig Tanzania

Espresso £2.20
Cappuccino £2.80
Latte £3.00
Flat white £2.80

MAP REF. 44

COFFEE 5 / 5 🫘🫘🫘🫘🫘   **OVERALL 4.75 / 5** ★★★★✬

The City

London's centre of finance and commerce may not boast the sheer number of cafés as Soho or the West End, but several recent high-profile openings have rapidly transformed its coffee fortunes. The City is surprisingly quiet at weekends (and many coffee bars open Monday to Friday only), so the area is best experienced during the bustling work week.

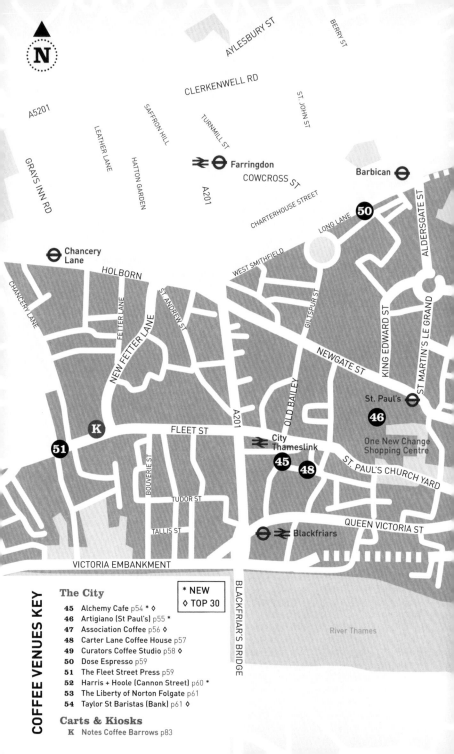

SCRUTTON STREET

CURTAIN ROAD

WHITECROSS ST

CITY ROAD

WILSON STREET

WORSHIP STREET

53

PRIMROSE ST

ECH ST

arbican

BISHOPSGATE

ELDON STREET

Moorgate ⊖ ⇄

FINSBURY CIRCUS

Liverpool
Street
⊖ ⇄

NDON WALL

LONDON WALL

MOORGATE

The City

OLD BROAD ST

HOUNDSDITCH

GRESHAM ST

54

47

EAPSIDE

POULTRY

Bank
⊖

LEADENHALL STREET

ansion
House
⊖

CANNON ST

49

FENCHURCH ST

52

Cannon Street ⊖ ⇄

Fenchurch Street ⇄

ER THAMES ST

Monument ⊖

WARK BRIDGE

LONDON BRIDGE

200   400m

Alchemy Cafe

8 Ludgate Broadway, EC4V 6DU

NEW

The Alchemists of old attempted to transform ordinary materials into precious metals. This City café is well practiced in espresso alchemy; extracting liquid gold with an array of coffee apparatus, including a cold brew drip tower. The Alchemy wizards also operate a roastery in South London, which has earned a reputation as one of the capital's best up and coming roasters. Customers interested in delving deeper into the mysteries of espresso science can join one of Alchemy's evening coffee courses.

+44(0)20 7329 9904
www.alchemycoffee.co.uk
◉ Blackfriars / ⇌ City Thameslink Rail

MON-FRI. 7:00am - 4:30pm
SAT-SUN. Closed

First opened 2013
Roaster Alchemy Coffee
Machine La Marzocco FB/80, 2 groups
Grinder Mazzer Robur E x2, Mazzer Super Jolly, Mahlkönig EK 43

Espresso £2.00
Cappuccino £2.50
Flat white £2.40

MAP REF. **45**

COFFEE 4.50 / 5

OVERALL 4.50 / 5 ★★★★✬

Artigiano St Paul's

1 Paternoster Square, EC4M 7DX

NEW

A dual-level coffee and wine bar near St Paul's Cathedral, Artigiano attracts City workers seeking more than just a habitual caffeine hit. Coffee is sourced from highly regarded Cornish roaster Origin Coffee, and prepared by a well trained barista team on a pair of custom-painted Lineas. Exposed brickwork and a contrasting grey and yellow design scheme create a striking backdrop. Go for lunch and you'll be hard pressed to resist the sandwiches, freshly prepared on-site with artisan bread.

+44(0)20 7248 0407
www.artigiano.uk.com
⊖ St Paul's

Sister locations Holborn

MON-WED. 7:00am - 8:00pm
THU-FRI. 7:00am - 8:00pm
SAT-SUN. 9:00am - 5:00pm

First opened 2013
Roaster Origin Coffee
Machine La Marzocco Linea, 2 groups x2
Grinder Mazzer Major x2

Espresso £1.80 / £2.00
Cappuccino £2.50 / £2.75
Latte £2.50 / £2.75
Flat white £2.50

MAP REF. **46**

COFFEE
4.25 / 5

OVERALL
4.50 / 5 ★★★★✫

Association Coffee

10-12 Creechurch Lane, EC3A 5AY

TOP 30

Association brings gourmet coffee and quality food from small suppliers to the heart of the City. A meticulously prepared range of pastries, cakes and sandwiches are served in sleek, yet accessible surroundings.

The interior follows a familiar industrial template, but adds City-influenced twists including a tiled communal table studded with banker's lamps, offering a great spot for meetings or casual lunches. Association's brew bar should not be missed, manned by professional baristas who are serious about their craft.

+44(0)20 7283 1155
www.associationcoffee.com
⊖ Aldgate / Liverpool Street

MON-FRI. 7:30am - 5:00pm
SAT-SUN. Closed

First opened 2012
Roaster Square Mile Coffee Roasters, Workshop Coffee Co. and guests
Machine Synesso Hydra, 3 groups
Grinder Mazzer Robur E, Mazzer Kony E, Mahlkönig Tanzania, Anfim Super Caimano

Espresso £2.20
Cappuccino £2.80
Latte £2.80
Flat white £2.80

MAP REF. **47**

COFFEE 4.75 / 5

OVERALL 4.75 / 5 ★★★★★

Carter Lane Coffee House

50 Carter Lane, EC4V 5EA

Nestled in one of London's narrowest streets, this pint-sized coffee bar means business. Sitting proudly on the immaculate counter is a high end Synesso Hydra, operated by well-trained Italian baristas. A small selection of pastries and toasted sandwiches compliment the coffee. The space may be small, but the lively staff create a convivial atmosphere in which to escape the city throng. Carter Lane successfully blends East End coffee expertise with a clean-cut style sharper than a city boy's lapels.

+44(0)20 7248 9493
www.carterlane-coffee.co.uk
⊖ St Paul's / ⇒ City Thameslink Rail

MON-FRI. 7:30am - 4:00pm
SAT-SUN. Closed

First opened 2012
Roaster Climpson & Sons
Machine Synesso Hydra, 2 groups
Grinder Mazzer Robur, Mazzer Mini

Espresso £1.30 / £1.50
Cappuccino £2.30
Latte £2.30
Flat white £2.30

MAP REF. **48**

COFFEE 4.50 / 5

OVERALL 4.25 / 5

Curators Coffee Studio

9a Cullum Street, EC3M 7JJ

There's a fine line between coffee and art at this small City café from former Kaffeine barista Catherine Seay. The vibrant turquoise La Marzocco Strada and matching grinders contrast with reclaimed wooden furniture and a vintage filing cabinet. Curators barista and artist, Tim Shaw, illustrates selected takeaway cups. The superb coffee is accompanied by irresistible cakes from Bittersweet Bakers and pastries from Yeast Bakery.

+44(0)20 7283 4642
www.curatorscoffee.com
⊖ Monument / Bank

MON-FRI. 7:30am - 5:30pm
SAT-SUN. Closed

First opened 2012
Roaster Nude Espresso, Square Mile Coffee Roasters
Machine La Marzocco Strada, 3 groups
Grinder Mazzer Robur E, Mazzer Mini, Anfim

Espresso £2.00
Cappuccino £2.80
Latte £2.80
Flat white £2.80

MAP REF. **49**

COFFEE 4.50 / 5

OVERALL 4.50 / 5 ★★★★✦

Dose Espresso

70 Long Lane, EC1A 9EJ

Straddling the border between the City and Farringdon, Dose Espresso is recognised as a leader in London's artisanal coffee scene. Owner and barista James Phillips sets a high standard in his small but welcoming espresso bar. All Dose coffee, milk and ingredients are ethically sourced and environmental consciousness is an important part of the company's identity. The café features a striking red, black and white colour scheme, which extends to the seductive curves of the Florentine FB/80 machine.

+44(0)20 7600 0382
www.dose-espresso.com
🚇 Barbican

MON-FRI. 7:00am - 5:00pm
SAT. 9:00am - 4:00pm
SUN. Closed

First opened 2009
Roaster Square Mile Coffee Roasters and guests
Machine La Marzocco FB/80, 3 groups
Grinder Ceado E92, Anfim Super Caimano, Mahlkönig Tanzania

Espresso £1.70 / £2.00
Cappuccino £2.80 / £3.00
Latte £2.80 / £2.90
Flat white £2.80 / £3.00   MAP REF. **50**

COFFEE 4.50 / 5   OVERALL 4.50 / 5 ★★★★✦

The Fleet Street Press

3 Fleet Street, EC4Y 1AU

The Fleet Street Press occupies a listed building complete with stunning stained glass window, and serves a mixed crowd of lawyers and students. Owners Davide Pastorino and Andy Wells oversee a friendly team pulling shots of Caravan coffee on a brand new La Marzocco. Expect top notch suppliers including non-homogenised milk from the Goodwood Dairy, and a healthy dose of witticisms dispensed to passers-by on what is surely London's most amusing pavement A-board sign.

+44(0)20 7583 7757
🚇 Temple

MON-FRI. 6:30am - 6:30pm
SAT-SUN. 10:00am - 5:00pm

First opened 2011
Roaster Caravan
Machine La Marzocco GB/5, 3 groups
Grinder La Marzocco Vulcano, Mazzer Mini, Mahlkönig Tanzania

Espresso £1.90
Cappuccino £2.30 / £2.60
Latte £2.30 / £2.60
Flat white £2.50   MAP REF. **51**

COFFEE 4.25 / 5   OVERALL 4.00 / 5 ★★★★☆

Harris + Hoole Cannon Street

113 Cannon Street, EC4N 5AW

NEW

Named after two coffee loving characters in the diaries of Samuel Pepys, Harris + Hoole is a new breed of coffee bar bringing artisan-style coffee to the high street. Founded by the Tolley siblings (owners of Taylor St Baristas), Harris + Hoole draws on a high level of coffee expertise and quality suppliers. This impressive flagship store is busy, yet runs efficiently thanks to well-trained staff and a digital ordering system. The company is set to replicate this success throughout the rest of the UK with an ambitious expansion programme.

+44(0)20 7621 0526
www.harrisandhoole.co.uk
⊖ Cannon Street / Bank

Sister locations Tooley Street / London Wall / King's Cross / Holloway Road

MON-FRI. 6:30am - 7:00pm
SAT-SUN. Closed

First opened 2013
Roaster Union Hand-Roasted
Machine Nuova Simonelli Aurelia II T3, 3 groups x4
Grinder Nuova Simonelli Mythos x8

Espresso £1.95
Cappuccino £2.30 / £2.60 / £3.00
Latte £2.30 / £2.60 / £3.00
Flat white £2.30 / £2.90 / £3.50

MAP REF. **52**

COFFEE
4.25 / 5

OVERALL
4.50 / 5

The Liberty of Norton Folgate

201 Bishopgate, Norton Folgate, EC2M 3UG

This café is named after a tiny self-governing area of East London that spanned just a few blocks up until 1855 and still gives its name to a short stretch of the A10. The narrow, sun-filled venue features a takeaway zone at one end and an eat-in area at the other. Custom-made lights inspired by the molecular structure of caffeine combine with a minimal black-and-white decor, high ceilings and huge windows to create a serene, crystalline space. Guest coffees and a variety of brewing methods are on offer.

www.libertyofnortonfolgate.co.uk
 Liverpool Street / Shoreditch High Street

Sister locations Department of Coffee and Social Affairs / Speakeasy Espresso & Brew Bar / Chancery Coffee / Tonic Coffee Bar

MON-FRI. 7:00am - 5:30pm
SAT-SUN. 10:00am - 4:00pm

First opened 2012
Roaster Climpson & Sons bespoke blend and guests
Machine La Marzocco FB/80, 3 groups
Grinder Mazzer Robur E x2, Mazzer Super Jolly, Mahlkönig Tanzania

Espresso £2.20
Cappuccino £2.70 / £2.90
Latte £2.70 / £2.90
Flat white £2.50

MAP REF. **53**

COFFEE 4.25 / 5   OVERALL 4.25 / 5

Taylor St Baristas Bank

TOP 30

125 Old Broad Street, EC2N 1AR

The recently refurbished Bank venue is one of the largest and busiest cafés in the Taylor St Baristas family. The sleek and spacious design includes lofty ceilings, timber finishing and designer drop lights that make this a great place for a business meeting or lunchtime escape. An on-site kitchen provides a scrumptious brunch and lunch service. The guest espresso changes every fortnight, and seasonal single origin coffees are served at the dedicated brew bar.

+44(0)20 7256 8665
www.taylor-st.com
 Bank / Liverpool Street

Sister locations Liverpool Street / Shoreditch / Canary Wharf / Monument / Mayfair / South Quay

MON-FRI. 7:00am - 6:00pm
SAT-SUN. Closed

First opened 2010
Roaster Union Hand-Roasted and guests
Machine Nuova Simonelli Aurelia T3 x2, 3 groups, Nuova Simonelli Appia, 3 groups
Grinder Mazzer Robur E x3, Ditting, Anfim x2

Espresso £1.80
Cappuccino £2.50 / £2.90
Latte £2.50 / £2.90
Flat white £2.50 / £3.40

MAP REF. **54**

COFFEE 4.50 / 5   OVERALL 4.50 / 5

The City

North

The fashionable boroughs of North London contain a huge variety of venues, from the colourful cafés of Camden – the rock 'n' roll hub of yesteryear – to chic neighbourhood delis in Islington. Moneyed Hampstead retains an English village style charm, just a short tube ride away from central London. Home to both busy professionals and counter-culture figures, the area's coffee culture reflects North London's diversity and fascinating history.

Caravan King's Cross

1 Granary Square, N1C 4AA

Inhabiting a monolithic former granary building, Caravan has graduated to the major league in both London's coffee and casual dining arenas. The unabashed use of concrete, and other reclaimed materials create an industrial atmosphere on a grand scale. The knowledgeable baristas are happy to offer advice on their seasonal blends, which are freshly roasted on the premises. The worldly food menu and wide range of coffees offer an excellent opportunity to experiment with coffee and food pairings.

+44(0)20 7101 7661
www.caravankingscross.co.uk
King's Cross

Sister locations Exmouth Market

MON-FRI. 8:00am - 11:30pm
SAT. 10:00am - 11:30pm
SUN. 10:00am - 4:00pm

First opened 2012
Roaster Caravan Coffee Roasters
Machine La Marzocco Strada EP, 3 groups,
La Marzocco Linea, 2 groups
Grinder Mazzer Robur E x4, Mahlkönig
Tanzania

Espresso £2.00
Cappuccino £2.60
Latte £2.60
Flat white £2.60

MAP REF. **55**

COFFEE 4.75 / 5   OVERALL 5 / 5

Coffee Circus Crouch End

136 Crouch Hill, N8 9DX

With its circus theme and vintage tearoom feel, Coffee Circus is a whimsical, friendly space in which to meet for coffee and cake. The business runs its own roastery operation, Mission Works Coffee, and customers can purchase beans directly from the café or have them ground to order. Coffee Circus also operates two takeaway sites: Coffee Wagon at Camden Stables Market and the quirky Grand Piano kiosk at Camden Lock Market.

+44(0)7507 551 472
www.coffeecircus.co.uk
⊖ Crouch Hill

Sister locations Coffee Wagon (Camden Stables Market) / Grand Piano (Camden Lock Market)

MON-FRI. 8:00am - 6:00pm
SAT-SUN. 9:00am - 6:00pm

First opened 2010
Roaster Mission Works Coffee
Machine Nuova Simonelli Aurelia, 2 groups
Grinder Mazzer Major E, Anfim, Mahlkönig Vario, Ditting

Espresso £1.80
Cappuccino £2.50
Latte £2.50
Flat white £2.50

MAP REF. **56**

COFFEE 4.25 / 5 🫘 🫘 🫘 🫘 ◖   **OVERALL** 4.25 / 5 ★ ★ ★ ★ ⯪

The Coffee Works Project

96-98 Islington High Street, N1 8EG

The Coffee Works Project owner Peter Theoklitou comes from a family of chefs and it shows. This stunning venue offers top-quality coffee and a fine deli menu. The centrepiece of the café is a beautiful Seattle-made Slayer espresso machine – the first of its kind in London. A variety of Has Bean seasonal roasts are available as espresso and on filter, complemented by a range of British cheeses and charcuterie. The Coffee Works Project is a fantastic addition to the London coffee scene and a must-visit destination.

+44(0)20 7424 5020
www.coffeeworksproject.com
⊖ Angel

MON-FRI. 7:30am - 6:00pm
SAT. 9:00am - 6:00pm
SUN. 10:00am - 5:00pm

First opened 2012
Roaster Has Bean
Machine Slayer, 3 groups
Grinder Mazzer Robur E, Anfim x2, Mahlkönig Tanzania

Espresso £2.00
Cappuccino £2.50
Latte £2.50
Flat white £2.50

MAP REF. 57

COFFEE 4.50 / 5
OVERALL 4.50 / 5 ★★★★½

The Fields Beneath

52 Prince of Wales Road, NW5 3NL

Named after Gillian Tindall's 1977 historical study of Kentish Town, this small speciality coffee outpost has already rallied a loyal local following. Owner Gavin Fernback, (previously of The Sandwich and Spoon) has converted a light-flooded railway arch at Kentish Town West station into a small but attractive coffee bar. The rotating coffee menu showcases up and coming British microroasters including Round Hill Roastery, Extract Coffee, Butterworth and many others.

+44(0)7912 435 754
⊖ Kentish Town West

MON-SAT. 7:30am - 6:00pm
SUN. 9:00am - 5:00pm

First opened 2012
Roaster Square Mile Coffee Roasters and others
Machine La Marzocco Linea, 2 groups
Grinder Anfim Super Caimano

Espresso £2.00
Cappuccino £2.50
Latte £2.60
Flat white £2.50

MAP REF. **58**

COFFEE 4.50 / 5   OVERALL 4.25 / 5 ★★★★☆

Ginger & White Belsize Park

2 England's Lane, NW3 4TG

Larger than its sister shop in Hampstead, Ginger & White Belsize Park was something of a happy accident - owners Tonia, Nicholas and Emma simply couldn't resist the high-ceilinged, sun-drenched corner venue when it became available. The café's kitchen supplies food to both Ginger & White stores. The large communal table is well-stocked with homemade peanut butter and preserves, while the cute upstairs area and outdoor tables are ideal spots to tuck into the moreish sandwiches and decadent cakes.

+44(0)20 7722 9944
www.gingerandwhite.com
⊖ Chalk Farm / Belsize Park

Sister locations Hampstead

MON-FRI. 7:30am - 4:30pm
SAT-SUN. 8:30am - 5:30pm

First opened 2012
Roaster Square Mile Coffee Roasters
Machine La Marzocco FB/80, 3 groups
Grinder Mazzer Robur E, Mazzer Mini

Espresso £2.20
Cappuccino £2.70
Latte £2.70
Flat white £2.70

MAP REF. **59**

COFFEE 4.50 / 5   OVERALL 4.25 / 5 ★★★★☆

Ginger & White Hampstead

4a-5a Perrin's Court, NW3 1QS

This proudly British café wears its heart on its sleeve. A local gem that is ever popular with the Hampstead community, Ginger & White serves well-crafted Square Mile coffee alongside modern British meals made using locally sourced produce. With the choice of a communal dining table, window seats or intimate leather sofas, this is a great place to enjoy a leisurely brunch.

+44(0)20 7431 9098
www.gingerandwhite.com
Hampstead

Sister locations Belsize Park

MON-FRI. 7:30am - 5:30pm
SAT-SUN. 8:30am - 5:30pm

First opened 2009
Roaster Square Mile Coffee Roasters
Machine La Marzocco FB/80, 3 groups
Grinder Anfim, Mazzer Robur E

Espresso £2.20
Cappuccino £2.90
Latte £2.90
Flat white £2.90

MAP REF. **60**

COFFEE 4.50 / 5   OVERALL 4.25 / 5 ★★★★

Leyas

20 Camden High Street, NW1 0JH

Camden High Street has long been the domain of coffee chain outlets, but this independent provides a welcome alternative. The spacious downstairs area is decorated by artwork and murals, and offers plenty of seating with mismatched tables and inviting chesterfield sofas. Leyas has upped the ante when it comes to coffee, installing a new machine, brew bar and cold drip tower. Guest espressos from the likes of Drop Coffee, Counter Culture and Notes Roastery contribute to the varied coffee menu.

www.leyas.co.uk
⊖ Mornington Crescent

MON-FRI. 7:30am - 5:30pm
SAT-SUN. 9:00am - 6:00pm

First opened 2011
Roaster Union Hand-Roasted and guests
Machine La Marzocco GB/5, 2 groups
Grinder Mazzer Robur E, Mazzer Super Jolly x2

Espresso £1.60
Cappuccino £2.20 / £2.50
Latte £2.20 / £2.50
Flat white £2.50

MAP REF. **61**

COFFEE 4.25 / 5　　OVERALL 4.25 / 5 ★★★★☆

Local Blend

587 Green Lanes, N8 0RG

NEW

Like an oasis in a desert of Turkish kebab houses and convenience stores, Local Blend finally brings speciality coffee to Harringay. The spacious Danish-inspired café feels like a living room, with comfy armchairs dotted around and a magazine stand overflowing with good reads. Owners Steve and Linda make you feel as though they are welcoming you into their own home. Climpson and Sons coffee and an array of sweet treats are served during the day, and a selection of wines, beers and cocktails are on offer in the evenings.

+44(0)20 8341 2939
www.localblend.co.uk
⊖ Turnpike Lane / Harringay Green Lanes

MON-THU. 8:00am - 10:30pm
FRI. 8:00am - 11:30pm
SAT. 9:00am - 11:30pm
SUN. 10:00am - 10:30pm

First opened 2013
Roaster Climpson & Sons
Machine La Marzocco Linea, 3 groups
Grinder Mazzer Super Jolly, Mazzer Mini, Ditting

Espresso £1.90
Cappuccino £2.50
Latte £2.30
Flat white £2.30

MAP REF. **62**

COFFEE 4.00 / 5　　OVERALL 4.25 / 5 ★★★★☆

Loft Coffee Company

4 Canfield Gardens, NW6 3BS

What Loft lacks in space, it compensates for with exceptionally friendly service, a welcome remedy to the scrum of Finchley Road. Sung-Jae Lee and his wife have created an uncomplicated, whitewashed space with warm wood panelling and a small number of tables. The Monmouth coffee is complemented by guest espressos such as Workshop 'Cult of Done'. Serving reliably excellent brews in an area not known for speciality coffee, Loft is a blessing for locals in search of a quality cup.

+44(0)20 7372 2008
⊖ Finchley Road

MON-FRI. 7:00am – 5:00pm
SAT. 8:00am – 4:00pm
SUN. 10:00am – 2:00pm

First opened 2012
Roaster Monmouth Coffee Company and guests
Machine La Marzocco Linea, 3 groups
Grinder Mazzer Major

Espresso £2.10
Cappuccino £2.60
Latte £2.60
Flat white £2.60

MAP REF. **63**

COFFEE 4.25 / 5   **OVERALL** 4.00 / 5 ★★★★☆

Maison d'Etre Coffee House

154 Canonbury Road, N1 2UP

This pretty café on the Highbury roundabout is a labour of love for owners Kim and Kostas, who gave up their day jobs to pursue a passion for food and coffee. Maison d'Etre serves a range of homemade cakes, sandwiches, treats and weekend brunch to an enthusiastic local crowd. Carefully selected suppliers include London Borough of Jam and Seven Seeded bakery. Hand-painted murals, vintage china and a welcoming atmosphere make this a serene spot to take five, particularly during the summer in the back garden.

+44(0)20 7226 4711
www.maisondetrecafe.co.uk
⊖ Highbury & Islington

MON-FRI. 7:30am - 7:00pm
SAT-SUN. 9:00am - 6:00pm

First opened 2011
Roaster Square Mile Coffee Roasters
Machine La Marzocco Linea, 2 group
Grinder Mazzer Major, Mazzer Super Jolly

Espresso £2.00
Cappuccino £2.40
Latte £2.40
Flat white £2.40

MAP REF. **64**

COFFEE 4.00 / 5   OVERALL 4.00 / 5 ★★★★☆

Melrose and Morgan Primrose Hill

42 Gloucester Avenue, NW1 8JD

This grocer and deli in leafy Primrose Hill is a cornucopia of beautifully prepared, locally sourced food. Homemade preserves fill the shelves, alongside a daily selection of seasonal salads, sandwiches, soups, cakes and treats. Breads and vegetables are also available, together with artisanal foods and a range of gourmet readymade meals. Look out for Melrose and Morgan's annual 'coffee month' when the deli runs free tasting events and other coffee-related activites.

+44(0)20 7722 0011
www.melroseandmorgan.com
⊖ Chalk Farm / Camden Town

Sister locations Hampstead

MON-FRI. 8:00am - 7:00pm
SAT. 8:00am - 6:00pm
SUN. 9:00am - 5:00pm

First opened 2004
Roaster Climpson & Sons
Machine La Marzocco Linea, 2 groups
Grinder Anfim

Espresso £1.60 / £1.85
Cappuccino £2.40
Latte £2.40
Flat white £2.40

MAP REF. **65**

COFFEE 4.25 / 5   OVERALL 4.00 / 5 ★★★★☆

Ruby Dock

Camden Market, Camden Lock Place, NW1 8AF

After the success of Lantana and Salvation Jane, the Australian team have opened their newest café in the heart of lively Camden Lock Market. Ruby Dock adds to the appeal of the area by bringing in specialty coffee and delicious small plates and cakes. It's an excellent place to catch a quick caffeine fix, rest weary feet and get some respite from the crowds. If you're in the mood for something stronger, the baristas will happily fix you a cocktail.

+44(0)20 7428 0421
⊖ Camden Town

Sister locations Lantana / Salvation Jane

MON-SUN. 9:00am – 5:30pm

First opened 2013
Roaster The Roasting Party
Machine La Marzocco Linea, 2 groups
Grinder Mazzer Robur E, Mazzer Super Jolly

Espresso £2.10
Cappuccino £2.60 / £2.90
Latte £2.60 / £2.90
Flat white £2.60

MAP REF. **66**

COFFEE 4.25 / 5

OVERALL 4.25 / 5 ★★★★☆

Tower 47

47 Chalk Farm Road, NW1 8AJ

Camden has long been a destination for exhilarating music, but its coffee scene has lagged behind its sister neighbourhoods like a woebegone groupie. Tower 47 is on a mission to put Camden back in the limelight.

The space incorporates a coffee bar, music shop, art gallery and a set of rehearsal rooms. An ensemble of London's rockstar roasters grace the coffee menu, served with plenty of New York style enthusiasm. Tower 47 draws on a shared love of coffee, music and the electric energy of Camden's streets.

+44(0)20 7482 2238
www.tower47.com
⊖ Chalk Farm

MON–FRI. 7:30am – 6:30pm
SAT–SUN. 9:00am – 6:30pm

First opened 2013
Roaster Volcano Coffee Works, Alchemy and guests
Machine La Spaziale S40, 3 groups
Grinder Mazzer Major, Mazzer Super Jolly, Mazzer Mini E, Ditting

Espresso £1.90
Cappuccino £2.50 / £2.75
Latte £2.50 / £2.75
Flat white £2.50 / £2.75

MAP REF. **67**

COFFEE 4.25 / 5   OVERALL 4.25 / 5

Vagabond N4

Charter Court, Stroud Green Road, N4 3SG

Vagabond adopts a wandering, nomadic approach to its coffee; Has Bean blends provide a top-quality base for a menu of beans sourced from roasters all over the world. Guest espressos and filter coffees vary frequently and offer a taste of the exotic in the otherwise sleepy Crouch Hill. A team of extremely friendly and passionate baristas man the coffee bar and bus a small number of tables both indoors and out.

+44(0)20 8616 4514
www.vagabondn4.co.uk
⊖ Finsbury Park / Crouch Hill

Sister locations Vagabond N7

MON–SUN. 7:00am – 7:00pm

First opened 2012
Roaster Has Bean
Machine Nuova Simonelli Aurelia II, 3 groups
Grinder Mazzer Super Jolly, Mahlkönig Vario

Espresso £1.80
Cappuccino £2.40
Latte £2.40
Flat white £2.40

MAP REF. **68**

COFFEE 4.50 / 5   OVERALL 4.25 / 5

Vagabond N7

105 Holloway Road, N7 8LT

NEW

With their second venue, the Vagabond boys have perfected the deliberately unfinished interior look. The pockmarked walls and weathered wooden floorboards create a delightfully grungy vibe, and the enormous back room plays host to lively unplugged gigs. There's also an inviting, if somewhat ramshackle, rear garden. The coffee is made with exceptional care, and single origins are available brewed by AeroPress or V60. Beans on offer come from an assortment of different roasters, so each visit promises something new.

⊖ Highbury & Islington

Sister locations Vagabond N4

MON–FRI. 7:00am – 6:00pm
SAT–SUN. 9:00am – 6:00pm

First opened 2013
Roaster Has Bean and others
Machine Conti Monte Carlo, 2 groups
Grinder Mazzer Super Jolly, Ceado, Nuova Simonelli MCD

Espresso £1.80 / £2.00
Cappuccino £2.40
Latte £2.40
Flat white £2.40

MAP REF. **69**

COFFEE 4.50 / 5   **OVERALL** 4.25 / 5 ★★★★☆

Wired 194

194 Broadhurst Gardens, NW6 3AY

After a short stint on West End Lane, Wired has found a new home on nearby Broadhurst Gardens. Bare steel, reclaimed wood and industrial fittings create an austere first impression, but settle in with a brew and the atmosphere is soon enriched by the chocolaty notes of Climpson & Sons coffee. If sweet things are your weakness, you'll find plenty to tempt you, including lemon and poppy seed cakes from The Flour Station bakery. Thankfully for West Hampstead locals, this time round Wired looks set to stay.

⊖ West Hampstead

MON-FRI. 7:30am - 5:00pm
SAT-SUN. 9:00am - 5:00pm

First opened 2013
Roaster Climpson & Sons
Machine Wega, 2 groups
Grinder Mazzer Super Jolly, Anfim

Espresso £1.80
Cappuccino £2.40
Latte £2.40
Flat white £2.40

North

NEW

MAP REF. 70

COFFEE 4.00 / 5

OVERALL 4.00 / 5 ★★★★☆

Carts & Kiosks

From neighbourhood farmers' markets to secluded city parks, London's coffee carts and kiosks caffeinate some of London's most captivating urban locations. Serving up coffee goodness in all weathers, these brave baristas are true heroes of the trade. Take the time to seek them out, and you'll soon discover a cadre of coffeeheads with fascinating stories to tell.

Bean About Town

Kentish Town Station, NW5 2AA

Carts & Kiosks

Bean About Town vans are a fixture on the streets of London, with six different outlets positioned at various points around town from Dalston to Clapham. The Kentish Town outlet has been doing business since 2005 and is a trusted favourite with locals and commuters seeking a quality caffeine hit. The Bean About Town ethos is all about quality and the personal touch, with well-trained baristas using lever machines to pull high-quality espresso for their loyal local customers.

+44(0)20 3239 6432
www.beanabouttown.com
⊖ Kentish Town

Sister locations Kensington Olympia / St. Katharine Dock / Dalston Kingsland / Clapham North / South Bank

MON–FRI. 7:00am – 4:30pm
SAT–SUN. 8:30am – 4:30pm

First opened 2005
Roaster Richard Jansz
Machine Izzo Pompei Lever, 3 groups
Grinder Anfim

Espresso £1.30 / £1.60
Cappuccino £1.80 / £2.20 / £2.50
Latte £1.80 / £2.20 / £2.50
Flat white £1.80 / £2.20

MAP REF. **A**

Blooming Good Coffee

Ezra Street, E2 7RH

Few places in London match Columbia Road market on Sundays for sheer sensory delight. The flower stalls are a riot of hues, the atmosphere alive with colourful market patter, and the air perfumed by hundreds of bobbing bouquets. Blooming Good Coffee adds the fruity notes of Square Mile espresso to the heady mix. The cheerful baristas encourage customers to photograph themselves against this vibrant backdrop with disposable cameras loaned from the stall. The best shots are shared on their Facebook page.

⊖ Hoxton

SUN. 8:00am – 2:00pm
MON–SAT. Closed

First opened 2002
Roaster Square Mile Coffee Roasters
Machine La Marzocco Linea, 3 groups
Grinder Anfim

Espresso £1.90
Cappuccino £2.40
Latte £2.40
Flat white £2.40

MAP REF. **B**

Coleman Coffee

Unit 5, Dockley Road, SE16 3SF

No trip to the artisan food producers of Spa Terminus is complete without a coffee from Coleman. Owner Jack has a refreshingly humble approach to his craft and a clear affinity with machinery, roasting beans with a restored 1950s Otto Swadlo roaster. The public can buy coffee and beans from the Saturdays-only stall located in Dockley Road Industrial Estate. Pull up a crate, order a cappuccino, and tuck into a pastry from neighbouring Little Bread Pedlar bakery.

+44(0)7809 496 695
www.colemancoffee.com
⊖ Bermondsey

SAT. 8:30am – 2:00pm
SUN–FRI. Closed

First opened 2011
Roaster Coleman Coffee
Machine La Marzocco Linea, 2 groups
Grinder Mazzer Super Jolly, Ditting

Espresso £1.50
Cappuccino £2.30

MAP REF. **C**

Craft Coffee Cart

The Ropewalk, Maltby Street Market, SE1 3PA

Splintering away from touristy Borough Market, the thriving set of artisan traders at Maltby Street Market are passionate about their produce. Craft Coffee is no exception. The baristas are committed to coffee excellence, rain or shine. Dosing carefully and extracting with precision, their attention to detail puts many bricks and mortar cafés to shame. After the success of the cart, owners Emily and Jamie established their first permanent coffee shop in Shoreditch.

⊖ Bermondsey / London Bridge

Sister locations Shoreditch

SAT. 9:00am – 3:00pm
SUN. 11:00am – 4:00pm
MON–FRI. Closed

First opened 2012
Roaster Notes Roastery
Machine Nuova Simonelli Appia, 2 groups
Grinder Mazzer Robur E, Mahlkönig Tanzania

Espresso £2.00
Cappuccino £2.40
Latte £2.60
Flat white £2.40

MAP REF. **D**

Daily Goods at Kinoko Cycles

Kinoko Cycles, 10 Golden Square, W1F 9JA

Kinoko Cycles (the reincarnation of Tokyo Fixed) is a handsome store full of alluring hand-crafted bicycles. Residing inside is a small coffee bar serving similarly enticing coffee. If you know your cranksets from your groupheads, there's a good chance you belong to the burgeoning ranks of London's coffee-loving cyclists, in which case Daily Goods should be a regular pit stop. The saddle-sore should leave their energy bars at home; the double shots served here will see you hurtling into the home counties.

⊖ Piccadilly Circus

MON-FRI. 8:00am - 6:00pm
SAT. 10:00am - 6:00pm
SUN. Closed

First opened 2013
Roaster Workshop Coffee Co.
Machine La Marzocco Linea, 2 groups
Grinder Anfim

Espresso £2.00
Cappuccino £2.70
Latte £2.70
Flat white £2.50

MAP REF. **E**

Dark Fluid

Brockley Market, Lewisham College Car Park, Lewisham Way, SE4 1UT

South London locals flock to Dark Fluid's Brockley Market stall on Saturdays for coffee hand-roasted by passionate coffeehead Lawrence Sinclair. The growing number of local independent cafés now serving Dark Fluid coffee is testament to the microroaster's success. Brockley Market is a destination in itself, with artisan producers offering a smorgasbord of fine foods, from vegetables to charcuterie, accompanied by several stalls serving hot fare.

+44(0)7984 886 723
www.darkfluid.co.uk
⊖ Brockley / ⇌ St. John's Rail

SAT. 10:00am - 2:00pm
SUN-FRI. Closed

First opened 2011
Roaster Dark Fluid
Machine Custom-built lever machine, 3 groups
Grinder Mazzer Major

Espresso £1.50
Cappuccino £2.50
Latte £2.50
Flat white £2.50

MAP REF. **F**

Espresso Base

St George's Churchyard, Bloomsbury Way, WC1A 2HR

Espresso Base nestles at the foot of St George's Bloomsbury, a magnificent church with English Baroque style architecture. The coffee cart is accompanied by a decking area with seating; the perfect spot for a sunny summer's day. Owner Gennaro is a charismatic Italian and coffee veteran with many years experience, and a story or two for those willing to listen. Himself a convert to third wave coffee, Gennaro's drinks are lovingly poured with finely textured milk and topped with beautiful latte art.

⊖ Holborn

MON-FRI. 8:30am – 4:30pm
SAT-SUN. Closed

First opened 2012
Roaster Has Bean
Machine La Marzocco FB/80, 2 groups
Grinder Mazzer Super Jolly, Mahlkönig Vario

Espresso £2.00
Cappuccino £2.50
Latte £2.50
Flat white £2.50

MAP REF. **G**

Giddy Up

Fortune Street Park, EC1Y 0SB

Just around the corner from the famous Whitecross Street Market is Fortune Street Park, a charming patch of green in the backstreets of the Barbican that hosts one of the best coffee carts in London. Owner Lee Harte's barista street smarts were honed at the legendary Pitch 42, Columbia Road and Flat Cap coffee stalls. This expertise is evident in the attention to detail found here and at the three sister carts.

⊖ Moorgate / Old Street

Sister locations Islington Memorial Green / Bep Haus / Newport Road Primary School

MON-FRI. 8:00am – 4:30pm
SAT-SUN. 10:00am – 4:00pm

First opened 2010
Roaster Square Mile Coffee Roasters, Has Bean
Machine La Marzocco GB/5, 2 groups
Grinder Anfim Super Caimano x2

Espresso £2.00
Cappuccino £2.60
Latte £2.60
Flat white £2.40

MAP REF. **H**

Merito Coffee

Swiss Cottage Farmers' Market, Eton Avenue, NW3 3EU

Merito Coffee is a welcome constant in an ever-changing London coffee landscape. Operating at the Swiss Cottage Market Mondays to Fridays, and the heaving Broadway Market on Saturdays, owner Jason Fitzpatrick and a hardy crew of baristas use both an espresso machine and pour over filters to make coffee for their loyal coterie of customers.

+44(0)7703 121 579
www.meritocoffee.com
⊖ Swiss Cottage

Sister locations Broadway Market
(Saturdays)

MON–FRI. 8:30am – 3:00pm
SAT–SUN. Closed

First opened 2007
Roaster The Coffee Plant and guests
Machine Elektra, 2 groups
Grinder Mazzer Royal

Espresso £1.20 / £1.50
Cappuccino £1.80 / £2.00 / £2.50
Latte £1.80 / £2.00 / £2.50
Flat white £2.00 / £2.50

MAP REF. **I**

Noble Espresso

Kings Cross Boulevard (at junction with Pancras Road), N1C 4T

NEW

There was a time when train station coffee conjured nightmarish images of dubious dark liquid in styrofoam cups. Thankfully those days are long gone. Commuters in North London can now pick up coffee expertly brewed by Shaun Young, former head barista at Kaffeine. Sited on Kings Boulevard outside redeveloped King's Cross station, the Noble Espresso cart is a saviour for red-eyed commuters. Part of the KERB street food collective, Noble Espresso is joined by other artisan food stalls trading Tuesday to Friday lunchtimes.

+44(0)7854 895 078
⊖ King's Cross St Pancras

MON–FRI. 7:00am – 3:15pm
SAT–SUN. Closed

First opened 2013
Roaster Notes Roastery bespoke roast
Machine La Marzocco Linea, 2 groups
Grinder Mazzer Kony E

Espresso £1.80 / £2.00
Cappuccino £2.40
Latte £2.40
Flat white £2.30

MAP REF. **J**

Notes Coffee Barrows

186A Fleet Street, EC4A 2HR

The polished wagons of Notes Coffee Barrows (formerly named Flat Cap Coffee) can be found dispensing fresh Notes espresso on weekdays at three locations across London. The Fleet Street cart nestles in the church courtyard of St Dunstan-in-the-West. Above the cart can be seen a magnificent seventeenth century clock, the first public clock to have a minute hand. Owned by well-respected coffee baron Fabio of Notes, the Notes carts are always a welcome sight around London and are synonymous with quality street coffee.

www.notes-uk.co.uk
⊖ Temple / Chancery Lane /
⇌ City Thameslink Rail

Sister locations St Giles / Borough Market

MON-FRI. 8:00am - 4:30pm
SAT-SUN. Closed

First opened 2009
Roaster Notes Roastery
Machine La Marzocco FB/80, 2 groups
Grinder Anfim

Espresso £1.40 / £2.00
Cappuccino £2.40 / £2.60
Latte £2.40 / £2.60
Flat white £2.40 / £3.00

MAP REF. **K**

Terrone & Co.

Netil Market, 13-23 Westgate Street, E8 3RL

Located in Netil Market (near Broadway Market), Terrone is possibly the only Italian third wave producer based in London. Originally from Salerno, enthusiastic owner Edy bucks the trend of the conservative Italian coffee fraternity with his lighter-roasted blends. The high standard of Terrone's coffee has already garnered plaudits, winning a gold star in the 2012 UK Great Taste Awards. Make the trip on a Saturday morning and wake up to an expertly poured Bianco Piatto (the Italian flat white).

www.terrone.co.uk
⇌ London Fields Rail

SAT. 10:30am - 5:30pm
SUN-FRI. Closed

First opened 2012
Roaster Terrone & Co.
Machine La Marzocco GB/5, 2 groups
Grinder Anfim

Espresso £2.00
Cappuccino £2.60
Latte £2.60
Flat white £2.40

MAP REF. **L**

Inner East

Brick Lane and Shoreditch provide London's creative pulse and are areas of tremendous diversity that have undergone rapid change in recent years. Many of the city's best new roasteries are based in East London and a range of artisan coffee venues provide fuel for the artists, students and urbanites who flock here for the weekend markets.

Handmade
in Milan, Italy.

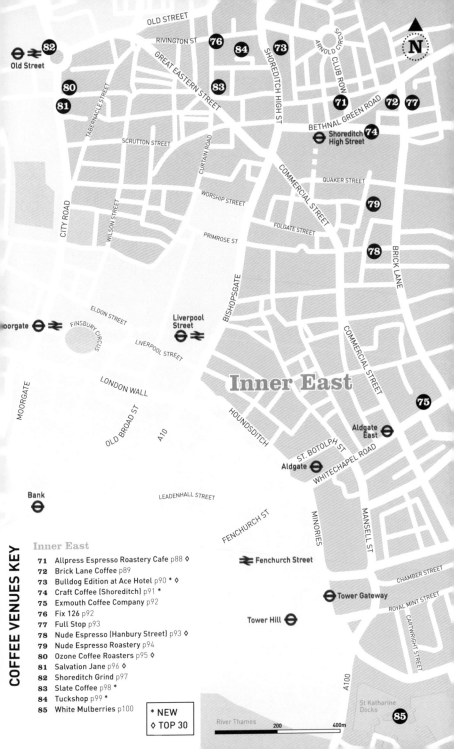

OLD STREET

RIVINGTON ST

GREAT EASTERN STREET

SHOREDITCH HIGH ST

ARNOLD CIRCUS

CLUB ROW

BETHNAL GREEN ROAD

Shoreditch
High Street

QUAKER STREET

BRICK LANE

COMMERCIAL STREET

FOLGATE STREET

PRIMROSE ST

BISHOPSGATE

ELDON STREET

FINSBURY CIRCUS

Moorgate

Liverpool
Street

LIVERPOOL STREET

LONDON WALL

Inner East

COMMERCIAL STREET

MOORGATE

OLD BROAD ST

A10

HOUNDSDITCH

Aldgate
East

ST. BOTOLPH ST

Aldgate

WHITECHAPEL ROAD

Bank

LEADENHALL STREET

FENCHURCH ST

MINORIES

MANSELL ST

Fenchurch Street

CHAMBER STREET

Tower Gateway

ROYAL MINT STREET

Tower Hill

CARTWRIGHT STREET

A100

St Katharine
Docks

River Thames   200   400m

TABERNACLE STREET

SCRUTTON STREET

CURTAIN ROAD

WILSON STREET

WORSHIP STREET

CITY ROAD

Old Street

N

Allpress Espresso Roastery

58 Redchurch Street, E2 7DP

Photo courtesy of the venue

This first UK venue for well-established New Zealand roastery Allpress Espresso has rapidly become a firm favourite in the heart of Shoreditch. The café's simple, natural interior focuses attention on the coffee itself, and a gleaming roaster is proudly on display. Allpress has had huge success in New Zealand and Australia, and is continuing its winning run in the UK, supplying many high-quality coffee shops and restaurants. Allpress has thrown out a challenge to the UK market and coffee lovers are reaping the rewards.

+44(0)20 7749 1780
www.allpressespresso.com
⊖ Shoreditch High Street

MON-FRI. 8:00am - 5:00pm
SAT-SUN. 9:00am - 5:00pm

First opened 2010
Roaster Allpress Espresso
Machine La Marzocco Linea PB, 3 groups
Grinder Mazzer Robur, Mazzer Super Jolly, Mahlkönig Tanzania

Espresso £2.00
Cappuccino £2.70
Latte £2.70
Flat white £2.70

MAP REF. **71**

COFFEE 4.75 / 5   🫘 🫘 🫘 🫘 🫘

OVERALL 4.50 / 5   ★ ★ ★ ★ ⯪

Brick Lane Coffee

157 Brick Lane, E1 6SB

Photo: Gary Handley

Situated at the northern end of Brick Lane, the headquarters of the Street Coffee mini-chain oozes alternative cool. The mish-mash of vintage furniture, eclectic wall art featuring pop-culture icons and the bicycles crammed inside create a youthful, urban feel.

Art students and East London locals linger on the couches, except on Sundays when Brick Lane Market turns this café into a heaving hub for bargain hunters. The company's twitter provides a constant stream of irreverent entertainment, but is not for the faint-hearted.

+44(0)20 7729 2667
www.streetcoffee.co.uk
🚇 Shoreditch High Street

Sister locations Goswell Road / Bermondsey Street

MON-SUN. 7:00am - 8:00pm

First opened 2001
Roaster Brick Lane Coffee
Machine Rancilio Classe 8, 3 groups
Grinder Mazzer Robur, Mazzer Royal, Mazzer Mini

Espresso £1.70 / £1.50
Cappuccino £2.20 / £2.50 / £2.80
Latte £2.20 / £2.50 / £2.80
Flat white £2.30 / £2.50

MAP REF. **72**

COFFEE 4.00 / 5	OVERALL 4.00 / 5

Bulldog Edition at Ace Hotel

100 Shoreditch High Street, E1 6JQ

NEW

Bulldog Edition is a collaboration between Square Mile Coffee Roasters and hip hotel group, Ace Hotel. The coffee bar opens into the lobby, providing ample seating and first-rate people watching opportunities. Drawing on the roaster's expertise, Bulldog presents an innovative coffee menu, including 'filter shots', strong filter-style coffee extracted with the espresso machine at low pressure. The knowledgeable baristas run a smooth service with impeccable attention to detail, setting a new quality benchmark for hotel coffee.

+44(0)20 7613 9800
www.acehotel.com/london
⊖ Shoreditch High Street / Old Street

MON-SUN. 6:30am - 6:00pm

First opened 2013
Roaster Square Mile Coffee Roasters
Machine La Marzocco Strada, 3 groups
Grinder La Marzocco Vulcano,
Mahlkönig EK 43

Espresso £2.00
Cappuccino £3.00
Latte £3.00
Flat white £3.00

MAP REF. **73**

COFFEE
4.75 / 5

OVERALL
4.50 / 5 ★★★★★

Craft Coffee Shoreditch

68 Sclater Street, E1 6HR

NEW

Owners Emily Fahey and Jamie Evans have a wealth of experience in London's speciality coffee scene, including stints at Notes and running their Maltby Street cart. Their first bricks and mortar café retains the minimalist feel of the former art gallery, but adds a downstairs seating area for a cosy space to hide away with a book. Craft serves exceptional coffee in one of the capital's most competitive coffee neighbourhoods, and often offers some unusual guest beans.

www.craft-coffee.co.uk

⊖ Shoreditch High Street

Sister locations Maltby Street Market

MON-FRI. 8:00am - 5:00pm
SAT-SUN. 10:00am - 5:00pm

First opened 2013
Roaster Notes Roastery
Machine La Marzocco Linea, 2 groups
Grinder Mahlkönig EK 43, Ceado E92

Espresso £2.00
Cappuccino £2.60
Latte £2.80
Flat white £2.60

MAP REF. **74**

COFFEE 4.50 / 5	OVERALL 4.25 / 5

Exmouth Coffee Company

83 Whitechapel High Street, E1 7QX

In a city now peppered with cool antipodean cafés, Exmouth offers a refreshingly eclectic mixture of East End and North African influences. Situated next to Whitechapel Gallery, this lively venue attracts a diverse, arty crowd. Roasted in-house, the coffee is dark and chocolaty. Food is freshly prepared in front of customers, and extraordinarily presented. The flatbread sandwiches, quiches, and sinfully sticky pecan brownies will keep you coming back for more.

⊖ Aldgate East / Aldgate

Sister locations Pitfield

MON-SUN. 7:30am - 8:00pm

First opened 2012
Roaster Exmouth Coffee Company
Machine La Marzocco Linea, 3 groups
Grinder Mazzer Robur E, Mazzer Super Jolly E

Espresso £2.00
Cappuccino £2.70
Latte £2.70
Flat white £2.70

MAP REF. **75**

COFFEE 4.00 / 5   OVERALL 4.25 / 5 ★★★★☆

Fix 126

126 Curtain Road, Shoreditch, EC2A 3PJ

The second Fix location in the heart of Shoreditch is a hub of creativity and a popular place for local creatives to meet and collaborate, or simply work alone on laptops or sketchbooks. This is also an excellent spot to stop for a daily caffeine fix, and friendly staff are happy to chat while whipping up a cup of custom-blended Climpson's espresso. A stool at one of the large front windows is the ideal place to sit and watch the comings and goings along vibrant Curtain Road.

+44(0)20 7033 9555
www.fix-coffee.co.uk
⊖ Old Street / Shoreditch High Street

Sister locations Fix

MON-FRI. 7:00am - 7:00pm
SAT-SUN. 8:00am - 7:00pm

First opened 2011
Roaster Climpson & Sons bespoke blend
Machine La Marzocco GB/5, 3 groups
Grinder Mazzer Robur E, Mazzer Super Jolly E x2

Espresso £1.50 / £2.00
Cappuccino £2.40 / £2.60
Latte £2.40 / £2.60
Flat white £2.40

MAP REF. **76**

COFFEE 4.25 / 5   OVERALL 4.00 / 5 ★★★★☆

Full Stop

202 Brick Lane, E1 6SA

Fittingly for its location, a vintage aesthetic predominates at Full Stop, with bench seats, Formica tables and comfy sofas furnishing a long, cosy space. However, the offering here is far from antique, with fresh gourmet sandwiches and cakes providing the perfect complement to the Square Mile coffee. Visit in the evening from Wednesday to Saturday for an interesting selection of craft beers and ciders, or tackle a weekend hangover with brunch and a Bloody Mary.

+44(0)20 7739 7086
🚇 Shoreditch High Street

MON-TUE. 7:30am - 6:00pm
WED-FRI. 7:30am - 9:00pm
SAT-SUN. 9:00am - 9:00pm

First opened 2011
Roaster Square Mile Coffee Roasters
Machine La Marzocco GB/5, 2 groups
Grinder Anfim x2

Espresso £2.00
Cappuccino £2.70
Latte £2.70
Flat white £2.70

MAP REF. **77**

COFFEE 4.00 / 5	OVERALL 4.00 / 5

Nude Espresso Hanbury Street   TOP 30

26 Hanbury Street, E1 6QR

Located close to the bustling Spitalfields and Brick Lane markets, Nude Espresso is one of London's busiest weekend destinations for coffee lovers. Nude offers much more than just a pit stop for weekend shoppers, with its famous 'East' espresso blend and filter options making it well worth braving the mobs any day of the week. The Nude Espresso Roastery itself is just around the corner on Brick Lane, for anyone who is interested to learn more about the coffee-making process.

+44(0)7712 899 335
www.nudeespresso.com
🚇 Shoreditch High Street / Liverpool Street

Sister locations Soho / Nude Espresso Roastery

MON-FRI. 7:00am - 6:00pm
SAT-SUN. 9:30am - 6:00pm

First opened 2008
Roaster Nude Coffee Roasters
Machine La Marzocco FB/80, 3 groups
Grinder Compak K-10 Professional x3

Espresso £2.00
Cappuccino £2.70
Latte £2.70
Flat white £2.70

MAP REF. **78**

COFFEE 4.50 / 5	OVERALL 4.75 / 5

Nude Espresso Roastery

The Cooperage Yard, Old Truman Brewery, 91-95 Brick Lane, E1 6QL

Photo courtesy of the venue

The Nude Espresso Roastery relocated to these premises after outgrowing its home at the Hanbury Street café. Just a short walk away on Brick Lane, this fresh and inviting space is where it all happens. Beans are roasted in small batches on a new 35kg Loring roaster, keeping Nude's three venues and a growing list of independent coffee bars well supplied. Visit to learn about the process of coffee selection, roasting and tasting from those who know it best, or simply to enjoy a coffee in an unusual space.

+44(0)7804 223 590
www.nudeespresso.com
⊖ Shoreditch High Street / Liverpool Street

Sister locations Soho / Hanbury Street

MON-FRI. 8:30am – 5:00pm
SAT-SUN. Closed

First opened 2008
Roaster Nude Coffee Roasters
Machine La Marzocco FB/80, 3 groups
Grinder Compak K-10 Professional x3

Espresso £2.00
Cappuccino £2.70
Latte £2.70
Flat white £2.70

MAP REF. **79**

COFFEE 4.50 / 5   OVERALL 4.25 / 5 ★★★★⭒

Ozone Coffee Roasters

11 Leonard Street, EC2A 4AQ

Photo: Gary Handley

Three years in the making, this huge dual-level roastery, café and bar is a stunning addition to London's coffee scene. A central island on the first floor contains an open kitchen, around which are arrayed bar stools where customers can sip a brew and watch their food being prepared. Further seating is provided downstairs, in view of the magnificent Probat roaster. Ozone's decor is a combination of Victorian industrial, Kiwi kitsch and South American barrio, resulting in a contemporary yet welcoming atmosphere that exudes an overarching passion for coffee.

+44(0)20 7490 1039
www.ozonecoffee.co.uk
⊖ Old Street

Sister locations Clipper Coffee Merchants

MON-FRI. 7:30am - 5:00pm
SAT-SUN. 9:00am - 4:00pm

First opened 2012
Roaster Ozone Coffee Roasters
Machine La Marzocco Strada, 3 groups, La Marzocco Linea, 3 groups
Grinder Mazzer Robur E x3, Mahlkönig EK 43, Mazzer Super Jolly E

Espresso £2.00
Cappuccino £2.80
Latte £2.80
Flat white £2.80

MAP REF. **80**

COFFEE 4.75 / 5   OVERALL 5 / 5   ★★★★★

Salvation Jane

1 Oliver's Yard, 55 City Road, EC1Y 1HQ

Salvation Jane takes its name from a beautiful flower that thrives in the Australian desert. This antipodean newcomer has helped transform East London's once arid coffee landscape into a blossoming caffeine community. A takeout bar serves those in a rush, and the large mid-century-inspired casual dining room is a fashionable spot for evening meals with cocktails. Salvation Jane's formidable brunch menu and potent Square Mile coffee are more than a match for even the most grievous Shoreditch hangover.

+44(0)20 7253 5273
www.salvationjanecafe.co.uk
⊖ Old Street

Sister locations Lantana / Ruby Dock

MON. 7:30am - 4:00pm
TUE-FRI. 7:30am - 10:00pm
SAT-SUN. 9:00am - 4:00pm

First opened 2012
Roaster Square Mile Coffee Roasters
Machine La Marzocco FB/80, 3 groups, La Marzocco Linea, 3 groups
Grinder Mazzer Robur E x2

Espresso £1.80 / £2.00
Cappuccino £2.60
Latte £2.60
Flat white £2.60

MAP REF. **81**

COFFEE 4.50 / 5

OVERALL 4.50 / 5

Shoreditch Grind

213 Old Street, EC1V 9NR

Photo: Gary Handley

With its retro cinema signage, circular interior and prime location right on the Old Street 'Silicon' roundabout, Shoreditch Grind is coffee theatre at its finest. Coffee lovers can sit on bar stools and look out at one of the city's busiest transport hubs while feeling insulated from the rat race with a cup of the delicious house blend in hand. As the Shoreditch night draws in, the café transforms into a hip bar serving beers, wines and cocktails. The venue also has a recording studio which is available for musicians to hire.

+44(0)20 7490 7490
www.shoreditchgrind.com
⊖ Old Street (Exit 8)

MON–THU. 7:00am – 11:00pm
FRI. 7:00am – 1:00am
SAT. 8:00am – 1:00am
SUN. 9:00am – 6:00pm

First opened 2011
Roaster Shoreditch Grind House
Espresso Blend
Machine La Marzocco Linea, 2 Groups x2
Grinder La Marzocco Vulcano x2

Espresso £2.10
Cappuccino £2.65 / £2.95
Latte £2.65 / £2.95
Flat white £2.65 / £2.95

MAP REF. **82**

COFFEE 4.25 / 5

OVERALL 4.50 / 5 ★★★★☆

Slate Coffee

96 Curtain Road, EC2A 3AA

Slate chalks up another win for speciality coffee in hipster-happy Shoreditch. The small, but punchy space is splashed with vivid graphics, completely in keeping with Curtain Road's edgy street art. Food arrives plated on slates, which perfectly match the custom painted stone grey La Marzocco espresso machine. If you prefer a mellow coffee, a rotating filter brew is also on offer. Slate has worked wonders with the space, and is proving a welcome addition to the area's creative coffee community.

+44 (0)20 3620 6980
www.slatecoffeelondon.co.uk
⊖ Shoreditch High Street / Old Street

MON-FRI. 8:00am - 7:00pm
SAT-SUN. 10:30am - 6:00pm

First opened 2013
Roaster Allpress Espresso
Machine La Marzocco FB/80, 2 groups
Grinder Mazzer Royal

Espresso £1.80 / £2.10
Cappuccino £2.80
Latte £2.80
Flat white £2.50

MAP REF. **83**

COFFEE 4.00 / 5

OVERALL 4.00 / 5 ★★★★☆

Tuckshop

471-473 The Arches, Dereham Place, EC2A 3HJ

Banish from your head any thoughts of mealy school fare; Tuckshop is a choice cut for coffee and delectable antipodean-inspired food. Opened by Australian chef Magnus Reid, Tuckshop is a simple, yet inspiring space softened by the flowing fonds of numerous potted plants. The café fronts the workspaces of White Rabbit Studios, and a large internal window affords a fascinating glimpse at the creative projects of the neighbouring workshop. Whilst Magnus oversees the food, coffee is expertly poured by Sam, formerly head barista at Nude Espresso.

+44(0)20 7729 3183
www.tuck-shop.co.uk
Old Street / Shoreditch High Street

MON-FRI. 8:00am - 6:00pm
SAT-SUN. 10:00am - 5:00pm

First opened 2013
Roaster Alchemy
Machine La Marzocco Linea, 2 groups
Grinder Compak K-10

Espresso £1.80
Cappuccino £2.00
Latte £2.00
Flat white £2.00

MAP REF. 84

COFFEE
4.25 / 5

OVERALL
4.25 / 5

White Mulberries

D3 Ivory House, St Katharine Docks, E1W 1AT

Like its namesake, White Mulberries is a sweet find; a rare combination of beautiful setting and great coffee. Located in St Katharine Docks - London's little-known marina - visitors have an enviable view of the swan-like sailboats. The café really comes into its own in fine weather when outdoor seating is provided overlooking the water. Customers have the option of Allpress Espresso, or single origin coffee brewed by AeroPress. Accompany your coffee with an award winning 'super moist' brownie.

www.whitemulberries.com
🚇 Tower Hill / Tower Gateway DLR

MON-FRI. 7:00am - 5:00pm
SAT. 8:00am - 6:00pm
SUN. 9:00am - 6:00pm

First opened 2012
Roaster Allpress Espresso and guests
Machine La Marzocco FB/80, 2 groups
Grinder Mazzer Major, Mazzer Super Jolly

Espresso £2.00
Cappuccino £2.60 / £2.90
Latte £2.50 / £2.80
Flat white £2.60 / £2.90

MAP REF. **85**

COFFEE 4.25 / 5

OVERALL 4.25 / 5 ★★★★✬

East

East London has successfully shaken off its label as a rough outer region to emerge as London's booming artistic neighbourhood. A wonderful combination of cultures and a thriving creative scene have helped put the area back on the map, and provide a fertile environment for London's coffee pioneers.

119 Lower Clapton

119 Lower Clapton Road, E5 0NP

(NEW)

Lower Clapton Road once attracted the unfortunate moniker 'Murder Mile' for its high rate of crime. Now the formerly unloved E5 postcode has received a visit from the gentrification fairy (along with an influx of creatives seeking reasonable rents). Thanks to the floor to ceiling windows and whitewashed walls, 119 feels infinitely light and airy. Local owner Erica Routledge has transformed the space into a quality neighbourhood café that longstanding and newly-arrived Clapton residents can all be rightly proud of.

+44(0)7780 784 696
www.119lowerclapton.co.uk
⊖ Hackney Central

MON-FRI. 8:00am - 5:00pm
SAT. 9:00am - 5:00pm
SUN. 10:00am - 5:00pm

First opened 2013
Roaster Workshop Coffee Co.
Machine Nuova Simonelli Aurelia II Digit
Grinder Mazzer Major, Mahlkönig Vario

Espresso £2.00
Cappuccino £2.40
Latte £2.50
Flat white £2.40

MAP REF. **86**

COFFEE 4.25 / 5

OVERALL 4.00 / 5 ★★★★☆

46b Espresso Hut

46b Brooksby's Walk, E9 6DA

Photo courtesy of the venue

Locals should seriously consider altering their morning commute expressly to visit 46b. Visitors from elsewhere will discover some of the best coffee served in Hackney in this unassuming, yet enchanting café. The zesty Red Brick blend pulled through the Seattle-made Synesso Cyncra is worth travelling for. Scrupulously selected suppliers include Northiam Dairy, E5 Bakehouse, and London Borough of Jam. 46b is Hackney's quietly brilliant venue.

+44(0)7702 063 172
www.46b-espressohut.co.uk
⊖ Homerton

MON-FRI. 7:30am - 6:30pm
SAT. 9:00am - 6:30pm
SUN. 10:00am - 6:00pm

First opened 2012
Roaster Square Mile Coffee Roasters
Machine Synesso Cyncra, 2 groups
Grinder Anfim Super Caimano, Mazzer Super Jolly

Espresso £1.90
Cappuccino £2.20
Latte £2.20
Flat white £2.20

MAP REF. **87**

COFFEE 4.50 / 5	🫘🫘🫘🫘🫘	OVERALL 4.25 / 5	★★★★⯪

Climpson & Sons

67 Broadway Market, E8 4PH

Photo: Gary Handley

Revered by coffee lovers in East London and beyond, the Climpson & Sons café has developed into one of the biggest names in London coffee. You'll be lucky to even make it through the door of the café while Broadway Market is in full swing on Saturdays.

The company's impressive new Loring roaster is housed nearby at Climpson's Arch on Helmsley Place. From Thursdays to Sundays, the roastery transforms into an informal drinking and dining venue, hosting supper clubs and summer barbecues.

+44(0)20 7812 9829
www.climpsonandsons.com
⊖ Haggerston / ⇌ Cambridge Heath Rail

Sister locations Broadway Market Stall (Sat only) / Climpson Arch (Thu-Sun)

MON-FRI. 7:30am - 5:00pm
SAT. 8:30am - 5:00pm
SUN. 9:00am - 5:00pm

First opened 2005
Roaster Climpson & Sons
Machine La Marzocco FB/80, 3 groups
Grinder Mazzer Robur x2, Mazzer Super Jolly x2

Espresso £1.60
Cappuccino £2.20 / £2.40
Latte £2.20 / £2.40
Flat white £2.20 / £2.40

MAP REF. **88**

COFFEE 4.50 / 5

OVERALL 4.50 / 5 ★★★★⯪

Cooper & Wolf

145 Chatsworth Road, E5 0LA

Occupying a sunny spot on gentrifying Chatsworth Road, Cooper & Wolf's Swedish charm is irresistible. Curious Scandinavian ornaments peep out from between potted plants, and lilting Nordic accents punctuate the atmosphere. Caravan coffee is exquisitely served by Alex and his baristas, while co-owner Sara heads up a kitchen offering delicious Swedish dishes, many from old family recipes. The råraka with Hansen & Lydersen salmon makes a particularly delicious accompaniment to a morning cappuccino.

www.cooperandwolf.co.uk
⊖ Homerton / ⇌ Clapton Rail

MON–THU. 9:00am – 5:30pm
FRI. 9:00am – 6:00pm
SAT–SUN. 10:00am – 6:00pm

First opened 2012
Roaster Caravan
Machine Synesso Cyncra, 2 groups
Grinder Mazzer Super Jolly, Anfim Super Caimano, Mahlkönig Tanzania

Espresso £1.60
Cappuccino £2.40
Latte £2.40
Flat white £2.40

MAP REF. **89**

COFFEE 4.25 / 5

OVERALL 4.25 / 5 ★★★★⭒

The Counter Café

Stour Space, 7 Roach Road, E3 2PA

The Counter Café is situated within Hackney Wick's Stour Space gallery, with a gorgeous view directly onto the canal. The smashed brick walls and signature vintage cinema seats lend the interior a grungy charm. The café roasts its own beans on a beautiful San Franciscan roaster, proudly displayed at the rear of the space. Nearby sister business, Crate Brewery, keeps local artists well supplied with craft beer and pizza. The Counter Café is a unique venue bursting with creative spirit; well worth the journey east.

+44(0)7834 275 920
www.thecountercafe.co.uk
⊖ Hackney Wick

Sister locations Crate Brewery

MON-FRI. 7:45am - 5:00pm
SAT-SUN. 9:00am - 5:00pm

First opened 2009
Roaster Counter Café Coffee
Machine Synesso Cyncra, 2 groups
Grinder Anfim

Espresso £1.80
Cappuccino £2.20
Latte £2.50
Flat white £2.20

MAP REF. **90**

COFFEE 4.50 / 5	OVERALL 4.50 / 5

Dreyfus

19 Lower Clapton Road, E5 0NS

NEW

Every walk of East London life is represented at this Hackney hangout. The clean Northern European-style decor mixed with a dash of Americana, such as the comfortable booth seating, create an easy-going environment. A mix of students, families, creative freelancers and the occasional canine come here for the reasonably priced - yet well made - coffee and hearty food. Egg stacks can be mixed and matched from a range of classics like Benedict, Royale or the more unconventional Leopold (the house special).

+44 (0)20 8985 4311
www.dreyfuscafe.co.uk
⊖ Hackney Central / ⇌ Hackney Downs Rail

MON. Closed
TUE-FRI. 8:00am - 7:00pm
SAT-SUN. 9:00am - 5:00pm

First opened 2012
Roaster Has Bean
Machine San Remo Verona, 2 groups
Grinder Mahlkönig K30 Vario

Espresso £2.00
Cappuccino £2.40 / £2.70
Latte £2.40 / £2.70
Flat white £2.40

MAP REF. **91**

COFFEE 4.00 / 5	OVERALL 4.00 / 5

Embassy East

285 Hoxton Street, N1 5JX

Behind the plain exterior and nondescript street address, Embassy East is a café with real soul. Opened on a modest budget, the visitor soon senses the love and ingenuity invested by the three founding friends (formerly of Flat White). It's the small things that make this Hoxton coffee bar special: the cleverly modified grinder, quirky pickle jar light fittings, and nostalgic cartons of Kellogg's cereal. The open kitchen also offers carefully prepared food made fresh with artisanal ingredients.

+44(0)20 7739 8340
www.embassyeast.co.uk
⊖ Hoxton

MON-FRI. 9:00am - 6:00pm
SAT-SUN. 10:00am - 6:00pm

First opened 2013
Roaster Workshop Coffee Co.
Machine La Marzocco Linea, 3 groups
Grinder Modified Anfim, Mahlkönig Columbia

Espresso £2.00
Cappuccino £2.50
Latte £2.70
Flat white £2.50

MAP REF. **92**

COFFEE 4.50 / 5	OVERALL 4.25 / 5
🫘🫘🫘🫘🫘	★★★★✫

Esters

55 Kynaston Road, N16 0EB

If you don't happen to live in Stoke Newington, a visit to Esters is likely to provoke serious envy for those fortunate enough to have such a brilliant little coffee shop on their doorstep. Standing on the site formerly occupied by café Fred & Fran, the new owners Nia and Jack have created a sanctum where everyone is welcome, from coffee geeks to mums. The food is outstanding, and the aforementioned coffee geeks will be delighted to sample two different filter coffees in addition to espresso-based drinks.

www.estersn16.com
⇌ Rectory Road Rail /
Stoke Newington Rail

MON. Closed
TUE-FRI. 8:00am - 5:00pm
SAT. 9:00am - 5:00pm
SUN. 10:00am - 4:00pm

First opened 2013
Roaster Has Bean
Machine La Marzocco Linea, 2 groups
Grinder Anfim, Mahlkönig EK 43

Espresso £2.20
Cappuccino £2.70
Latte £2.80
Flat white £2.70

MAP REF. **93**

COFFEE 4.50 / 5

OVERALL 4.25 / 5 ★★★★✫

Fabrica 584

584 Kingsland Road, E8 4AH

Owner Roberto's Italian sensibilities make this café a satisfying alternative to the usual laidback style of Kiwi and Aussie-owned coffee bars. The industrial interior is furnished with mismatched tables and chairs, and softly illuminated by low-hanging lamps. The space gives way to a large outdoor area, which forms a glorious suntrap in summer. The vintage Faema machine at the heart of the operation adds serious retro appeal to this cool Dalston hangout.

+44(0)20 7998 8041
⊖ Dalston Junction

MON-FRI. 8:30am - 7:00pm
SAT. 9:30am - 7:00pm
SUN. 10:00am - 6:00pm

First opened 2011
Roaster Monmouth Coffee Company
Machine Faema E61, 2 groups
Grinder Mazzer Super Jolly

Espresso £1.60
Cappuccino £2.60
Latte £2.60
Flat white £2.60

MAP REF. **94**

COFFEE
4.25 / 5

OVERALL
4.50 / 5 ★★★★☆

Fabrique Bakery

Arch 385, Geffrye Street, E2 8HZ

NEW

Bakery café Fabrique is a cinnamon-sprinkled slice of Stockholm nestled in a railway arch near Hoxton station. The Swedish coffee break, known as fika, is a national institution almost always involving baked goods, and the sweeter the better. So it's just as well that Fabrique's artisan bakers are revered for their decadent buns, bejewelled with sugar crystals and doused with cinnamon or cardamom. The coffee is crafted with beans from Johan & Nyström, a highly respected Nordic artisan roaster.

+44(0)20 7033 0268
www.fabrique.co.uk
⊖ Hoxton

MON-FRI. 8:00am - 6:00pm
SAT-SUN. 10:00am - 6:00pm

First opened 2012
Roaster Johan & Nyström
Machine Dalla Corte, 3 groups
Grinder Mahlkönig K30

Espresso £1.75 / £2.00
Cappuccino £2.50 / £2.75
Latte £2.75
Flat white £2.50 / £2.75

MAP REF. **95**

COFFEE
3.75 / 5

OVERALL
4.00 / 5
★ ★ ★ ★ ☆

G&T

204 Cambridge Heath Road, E2 9NQ

This tiny coffee house and deli is the passion project of Italian couple Marco and Ilaria, who serve lovingly prepared Has Bean coffee to the artists and passersby on busy Cambridge Heath Road. G&T also offers a carefully selected range of organic, locally sourced produce and vegan foods. Cakes and pastries sit alongside bottles of Italian pasta sauce, preserves and artisanal bread baked just up the road at E5 Bakehouse.

+44(0)7956 355 145
www.gandtlondon.co.uk
≥ Cambridge Heath Rail /
⊖ Bethnal Green

MON-FRI. 8:00am - 4:00pm
SAT-SUN. 9:00am - 4:00pm

First opened 2011
Roaster Has Bean and guests
Machine Rancilio Classe 9 Xcelsius, 2 groups
Grinder Anfim Super Caimano, Mahlkönig Vario

Espresso £2.00
Cappuccino £2.50
Latte £2.50
Flat white £2.50

MAP REF. **96**

COFFEE 4.25 / 5	OVERALL 4.00 / 5

Grind Coffee Bar Westfield Stratford City

Lower ground floor, Westfield Stratford, E20 1EJ

A vast shopping mall is the last place you'd expect to find great coffee, but tucked away down one end of Westfield Stratford is an outpost of Putney café Grind. The venue occupies a large, open-plan space designed to provide a respite from the bedlam of the shopping mall with kitchen-style tables, leather wingback chairs and a soothing New Zealand theme. Coffee is tailored for busy shoppers but more serious options are also available in the form of guest espressos and single-origin filters.

www.grindcoffeebar.co.uk
⊖ Stratford

Sister locations Putney

MON-FRI. 8:00am - 9:00pm
SAT. 9:00am - 9:00pm
SUN. 11:00am - 6:00pm

First opened 2011
Roaster London Coffee Roasters
Machine La Marzocco Strada EP, 3 groups
Grinder Mazzer Robur x2

Espresso £1.80
Cappuccino £2.30 / £2.70 / £2.90
Latte £2.30 / £2.70 / £2.90
Flat white £2.30 / £2.70 / 2.90

MAP REF. **97**

COFFEE 4.25 / 5	OVERALL 4.25 / 5

The Hackney Pearl

11 Prince Edward Road, E9 5LX

Hidden away in the Hackney Wick industrial area, The Hackney Pearl rewards the urban explorer with simple, yet delicious coffee and food. The Pearl serves as a hub for the growing community of local artists, many of whom work in studios nearby. The broad glass shopfront admits plenty of natural light, and outdoor seating is also plentiful.
The beautiful seasonal menu changes daily and an extensive bar list is also available. The Pearl is open until late every evening for dinner, drinks and events.

+44(0)20 8510 3605
www.thehackneypearl.com
⊖ Hackney Wick

MON-SAT. 10:00am - 11:00pm
SUN. 10:00am - 8:00pm

First opened 2009
Roaster Ozone Coffee Roasters
Machine La Marzzoco FB/80, 3 groups
Grinder Mazzer Major, Mazzer Super Jolly

Espresso £1.80 / £2.10
Cappuccino £2.00 / £2.50
Latte £2.00 / £2.50
Flat white £2.00 / £2.50

MAP REF. **98**

COFFEE 4.00 / 5   OVERALL 4.00 / 5 ★★★★☆

Haggerston Espresso Room

Unit C, 13 Downham Road, N1 5AA

Haggerston Espresso Room, or HER as this Dalston darling likes to be known, is a sweetheart of the Hackney creative brigade. The mismatched furniture is a combination of school classroom and grandmother chic, which is sure to suit East End fashionistas down to the ground (quite literally; the sofas boast considerable sag). Fortunately the Climpson's coffee is no slouch, and the 'sexy toast' contributes to a seductive food menu. HER is a characterful café with a sense of humour you can't help but like.

+44(0)20 7249 0880
⊖ Haggerston

MON-FRI. 7:30am - 6:00pm
SAT. 9:00am - 6:00pm
SUN. 10:00am - 6:00pm

First opened 2011
Roaster Climpson & Sons
Machine La Marzocco Linea, 3 groups
Grinder Mazzer Royal, Mazzer Super Jolly

Espresso £2.00
Cappuccino £2.50 / £2.90
Latte £2.50 / £2.90
Flat white £2.50

MAP REF. **99**

COFFEE 4.00 / 5   OVERALL 4.00 / 5 ★★★★☆

Look Mum No Hands! Hackney

125-127 Mare Street, E8 3RH

More commuters choose to cycle than drive to work in Hackney. As one of its main arteries, Mare Street at times resembles a stage from Le Tour de France. It's the perfect location then, for the second Look Mum No Hands! cycle-themed café. With more space on the bar, there's a greater range of coffees on offer than at the first Old Street venue. What's more, there's a particularly tempting line up of craft beers on tap, although cyclists may want to sober up with an espresso before returning to Mare Street's traffic madness.

+44(0)7985 200 472
www.lookmumnohands.com
London Fields Rail

Sister locations Clerkenwell

MON-FRI. 8:00am - 10:00pm
SAT. 9:00am - 10:00pm
SUN. 9:30am - 10:00pm

First opened 2013
Roaster Square Mile Coffee Roasters and guests
Machine Kees van der Westen Mirage, 3 groups
Grinder Anfim Barista x2, Mahlkönig Vario

Espresso £2.00
Flat white £2.60

MAP REF. **100**

COFFEE 4.50 / 5	OVERALL 4.25 / 5

MacIntyre Coffee

19-21 Hoxton Street, N1 6NG

NEW

Established in a stripped-back former garage, MacIntyre Coffee embodies Shoreditch's DIY spirit. Owner Alex MacIntyre places emphasis on innovation and experimentation, and is currently developing a custom coffee grinder. The distinctive coffee bar designed by espresso entrepreneur Hoi Chi Ng of Coming Soon Coffee, supports two low-profile Speedster machines. This is an excellent place to discover the latest developments in espresso extraction and coffee equipment.

⊖ Old Street

MON-FRI. 7:30am – 5:30pm
SAT. 9:00am – 4:00pm
SUN. Closed

First opened 2013
Roaster Workshop Coffee Co. and guests
Machine Kees van der Westen Mirage Speedster, 1 group x2
Grinder Mahlkönig EK 43

Espresso £2.00
Cappuccino £2.50
Latte £2.50
Flat white £2.50

MAP REF. **101**

COFFEE 4.50 / 5

OVERALL 4.25 / 5 ★★★★✫

Mouse & De Lotz

103 Shacklewell Lane, E8 2EB

To enter Mouse & De Lotz is to step back in time to an era of glass milk bottles, Singer sewing machines and cakes made by hand. Squashy sofas, window seats and a pretty, vintage aesthetic enhance the comforting retro feel, but free wifi brings this café right up to date and makes it an ideal place to spend a lazy hour. Superb coffee is prepared by a rotating staff of artists, students and parents, all of whom bring full-time passion to the food and drinks they prepare for their Dalston customers.

+44(0)20 3489 8082
www.mousedelotz.com
⊖ Dalston Kingsland

MON–FRI. 8:00am – 5:00pm
SAT. 9:00am – 5:00pm
SUN. 10:00am – 5:00pm

First opened 2010
Roaster Square Mile Coffee Roasters
Machine La Marzocco Linea, 2 groups
Grinder Mazzer Super Jolly E, Anfim

Espresso £2.00
Cappuccino £2.40
Latte £2.40
Flat white £2.40

MAP REF. 102

COFFEE 4.00 / 5   🫘 🫘 🫘 🫘 🫘

OVERALL 4.00 / 5   ★ ★ ★ ★ ☆

Muff Customs Cafe

4c Roach Road, E3 2PA

NEW

Swaggering into the creative hotbed of Hackney Wick, Muff Customs is a café and motorcycle workshop. If it has two wheels and makes a loud noise, they're interested. However, the Muff Customs Cafe (short for exhaust muffler, in case you were wondering) is a surprisingly tranquil setting to enjoy a coffee. Housed in a separate building from the workshop, it's a laid-back space adorned with custom motorcycle memorabilia. Like its souped-up creations, this café boasts a genuinely unique character you won't find elsewhere.

www.muffcustoms.com
⊖ Hackney Wick

MON–FRI. 8:00am – 5:00pm
SAT. 9:00am – 5:00pm
SUN. 9:00am – 4:00pm

First opened 2013
Roaster The Counter Café bespoke blend
Machine Ibital, 2 groups
Grinder San Remo

Espresso £1.60
Cappuccino £2.30
Latte £2.30
Flat white £2.20

MAP REF. 103

COFFEE 3.75 / 5   OVERALL 4.00 / 5 ★★★★☆

Pavilion

Victoria Park, Crown Gate West, E9 7DE

Perfectly positioned overlooking a beautiful lake, Pavilion offers excellent coffee and fresh food to the crowds of locals who flock to Victoria Park every day to walk their dogs, exercise, spend time with family or simply relax. The café itself features a striking domed glass roof and the outdoor decking area offers stunning views over the lake and park. Pavilion's popular brunch menu is organic and locally sourced wherever possible. The British-style fare is best sampled on a sunny weekend, so arrive early to avoid the queue.

+44(0)20 8980 0030
www.the-pavilion-cafe.com
⊖ Bethnal Green / Mile End

Sister locations Elliots

MON–SUN. 8:00am – 4:00pm

First opened 2007
Roaster Square Mile Coffee Roasters
Machine Synesso Cyncra, 3 groups
Grinder Mazzer Robur, Mazzer Super Jolly

Espresso £2.00
Cappuccino £2.20
Latte £2.50
Flat white £2.40

MAP REF. **104**

COFFEE 4.25 / 5 🫘 🫘 🫘 🫘 ◖ | OVERALL 4.25 / 5 ★ ★ ★ ★ ☆

Railroad

120-122 Morning Lane, E9 6LH

A visit to Railroad is food for both the body and the mind - the delicious and inventive seasonal menu (produced as if by magic from a tiny kitchen) is complemented by a small range of books for sale. Square Mile coffee is served in handmade earthenware cups that lend themselves to being held in both hands on cold days. The café's sunny corner location makes it an ideal spot to sit and bask in the sunshine.

+44(0)20 8985 2858
www.railroadhackney.co.uk
⊖ Hackney Central / Homerton

MON–TUE. Closed
WED–FRI. 10:00am – 11:00pm
SAT. 10:00am – 11:00pm
SUN. 10:00am – 5:00pm

First opened 2010
Roaster Square Mile Coffee Roasters
Machine Nuova Simonelli, 2 groups
Grinder Anfim, Mazzer Mini

Espresso £2.00 / £2.20
Cappuccino £2.40 / £2.60
Latte £2.40 / £2.60
Flat white £2.40 / £2.60

MAP REF. **105**

COFFEE 4.00 / 5 🫘 🫘 🫘 🫘 ◔ | OVERALL 4.00 / 5 ★ ★ ★ ★ ☆

Reilly Rocket

507 Kingsland Road, E8 4AU

Situated behind a motorcycle shop, Reilly Rocket is the antidote to twee, chintzy cafés and industrial chic. Decorated with colourful memorabilia, brown leather sofas, taxidermy and graphic wall art, Reilly's is a haven for lovers of rebellion and retro road culture. Hunter S. Thompson would have been right at home here. The coffee is just as gutsy and is pulled by a team of hardcore baristas. If you're in need of further fuel, the Antipodean-inspired brunch menu will soon have you firing on all cylinders.

www.reillyrocket.com
⊖ Dalston Junction

MON–FRI. 8:00am – 5:00pm
SAT. 9:00am – 5:00pm
SUN. 10:00am – 5:00pm

First opened 2011
Roaster Square Mile Coffee Roasters
Machine La Marzocco Linea, 2 groups
Grinder Anfim

Espresso £1.80
Cappuccino £2.60
Latte £2.50
Flat white £2.50

MAP REF. 106

COFFEE 4.25 / 5   OVERALL 4.25 / 5 ★★★★½

Taylor St Baristas Canary Wharf

8 South Colonnade, Canary Wharf, E14 4PZ

This lean, mean café is designed to produce a high volume of quality coffee for the district's bankers and business people. The venue is predominantly set up to serve takeaway drinks, but there are also a small number of tables. Customers can also opt for a single origin coffee brewed by AeroPress. A full breakfast and brunch menu is on offer complemented by cakes and Australian classics such as lamingtons, and cheese and Vegemite muffins.

+44(0)20 7519 6536
www.taylor-st.com
⊖ Canary Wharf

Sister locations New Street / Shoreditch / Monument / Bank / Mayfair / South Quay

MON–FRI. 7:00am – 6:00pm
SAT–SUN. Closed

First opened 2011
Roaster Union Hand-Roasted and guests
Machine Nuova Simonelli Aurelia II, 3 groups x2, Synesso Cyncra, 2 groups
Grinder Mazzer Robur E x2, Mazzer Major E x2, Anfim, Mahlkönig Tanzania

Espresso £1.80
Cappuccino £2.50 / £2.90
Latte £2.50 / £2.90
Flat white £2.50 / £3.40

MAP REF. 107

COFFEE 4.50 / 5   OVERALL 4.25 / 5 ★★★★½

Wilton Way Café

63 Wilton Way, E8 1BG

Wilton Way Café combines superb coffee and fresh, simple food with art and music to create a memorable experience. Incorporating clever modular furniture, rotating art exhibits, a busy coffee bar, a generous display of cakes and treats and a radio corner for live local broadcasts, Wilton's makes excellent use of its intimate but vibrant space. Visit on a sunny Saturday to enjoy a fine cup of coffee on the footpath outside, along with the crowds of the Wilton Way faithful.

+44(0)20 7249 0444
www.londonfieldsradio.co.uk/the-cafe
⊖ Hackney Central /
⇌ Hackney Downs Rail

MON-FRI. 8:00am - 5:00pm
SAT. 8:00am - 6:00pm
SUN. 9:00am - 6:00pm

First opened 2009
Roaster Climpson & Sons
Machine La Marzocco Linea, 2 groups
Grinder Mazzer Super Jolly, Anfim

Espresso £1.50 / £1.80
Cappuccino £2.30 / £2.50
Latte £2.30 / £2.50
Flat white £2.30 / £2.50

MAP REF. 108

COFFEE 4.25 / 5	🫘🫘🫘🫘🫘	OVERALL 4.50 / 5	★★★★✦

Zealand Road Coffee

391 Roman Road, E3 5QS

Roman Road seems an unlikely place to hunt for a good coffee. Located just a short walk away from leafy Victoria Park, Zealand Road Coffee's corner location is a natural sun trap and the creative locals take advantage of the laid-back atmosphere to catch up on work or a good novel. Beans are supplied by Cornwall-based Origin Coffee, which has justly earned a reputation as one of the UK's premier small batch roasters. Origin's coffee is relatively uncommon in London and worth seeking out.

+44(0)7940 235 493
⊖ Mile End / Bethnal Green

MON-SAT. 8:00am - 5:00pm
SUN. 9:00am - 5:00pm

First opened 2011
Roaster Origin Coffee
Machine La Marzocco Linea, 2 groups
Grinder Mazzer Major, Compak K6

Espresso £1.50
Cappuccino £2.20 / £2.40
Latte £2.20 / £2.40
Flat white £2.20

MAP REF. 109

COFFEE 4.25 / 5	🫘🫘🫘🫘🫘	OVERALL 4.00 / 5	★★★★☆

121

South East

One of the capital's best kept secrets, South East London is home to a small number of quietly brilliant coffee venues, and is rapidly establishing itself on the coffee map. With the completion of the Overground line from East London to Clapham Junction via Peckham, the area is now more accessible, and rewards the urban explorer with a vibrant foodie and market scene.

Anderson & Co

139 Bellenden Road, SE15 4DH

Anderson & Co was one of the first places to offer speciality coffee in a neighbourhood now in the throes of a foodie revolution. The café-restaurant complements its coffee with artisan breads, cakes, pastries and small range of craft beer. The white, bright interior serves as a perfect canvas for the medley of tastes on offer. Tantalising aromas waft from the open kitchen to the secluded outdoor seating area at the rear. With the new Overground link, there's never been a better time to explore Peckham's thriving café culture.

+44(0)20 7469 7078
www.andersonandcompany.wordpress.com
⊖ Peckham Rye

MON–SAT. 8:00am – 5:00pm
SUN. 8:30am – 4:30pm

First opened 2011
Roaster Square Mile Coffee Roasters
Machine La Marzocco Linea, 2 groups
Grinder Mazzer Super Jolly, Anfim

Espresso £1.75
Cappuccino £2.50
Latte £2.50
Flat white £2.50

MAP REF. 110

COFFEE 4.25 / 5   OVERALL 4.25 / 5

Arlo & Moe

340 Brockley Road, SE4 2BT

Arlo & Moe is a simply beautiful little neighbourhood café tucked away to the south of Brockley. Since opening it has struck a chord with the locals; staff and customers mingle freely as cheerful rockabilly tunes fill the air, and children are particularly welcomed. The coffee is locally roasted by Dark Fluid, and accompanied by a tempting food menu. Try the signature 'sexy toast' on campaillou bread, or meet some new friends at one of Arlo & Moe's supper nights.

+44(0)7749 667 207
⇌ Crofton Park Rail

MON–FRI. 7:30am – 4:00pm
SAT–SUN. 10:00am – 4:00pm

First opened 2012
Roaster Dark Fluid
Machine Gaggia, 2 groups
Grinder La Spaziale Astro

Espresso £1.60
Cappuccino £2.40 / £3.00
Latte £2.40 / £3.00
Flat white £2.40

MAP REF. 111

COFFEE 3.75 / 5   OVERALL 4.00 / 5

Browns of Brockley

5 Coulgate Street, SE4 2RW

Browns of Brockley is top dog for coffee in South London. Well-trained staff pull shots on a La Marzocco Strada, and offer single origins on filter. The simple layout and natural colour scheme create a calming atmosphere. Owner Ross Brown is committed to sourcing the highest quality ingredients for both coffee and food. Local suppliers include Flock & Herd butchers and Blackwood Cheese, whilst Northiam Dairy supplies deliciously sweet milk. The friendly team is completed by Ludd the pug, Browns' lovable canine mascot.

+44(0)20 8692 0722
www.brownsofbrockley.com
⊖ Brockley

MON-FRI. 7:30am - 6:00pm
SAT. 9:00am - 5:00pm
SUN. 10:00am - 4:00pm

First opened 2009
Roaster Square Mile Coffee Roasters
Machine La Marzocco Strada EP, 2 groups
Grinder Mazzer Robur E x2

Espresso £2.00
Cappuccino £3.00
Latte £3.20
Flat white £3.00

MAP REF. 112

COFFEE
4.50 / 5   🫘 🫘 🫘 🫘 🫘

OVERALL
4.50 / 5   ★ ★ ★ ★ ☆

125

Café Viva

44 Choumert Road, SE15 4SE

Choumert Road is a true microcosm of South East London. Café Viva squeezes between tranquil Victorian terraces and the colourful mêlée of Rye Lane's African food shops. Volcano Coffee is lovingly served in 70s cups, and tea brewed in owner Lily's collection of Brown Betty teapots. Herself a Goldsmiths College graduate, Lily hosts pieces from local artists, alongside framed messages from Peckham's post-riot 'Peace Wall'. At Café Viva terrific coffee and a strong sense of community go hand in hand.

+44(0)7918 653 533
www.cafeviva.co.uk
⊖ Peckham Rye

MON. Closed
TUE-FRI. 7:30am - 5:00pm
SAT-SUN. 9:00am - 5:00pm

First opened 2012
Roaster Volcano Coffee Works
Machine La Marzocco Linea, 2 groups
Grinder Mazzer Super Jolly

Espresso £1.80
Cappuccino £2.50
Latte £2.50
Flat white £2.50

MAP REF. **113**

COFFEE 4.00 / 5   **OVERALL** 4.00 / 5 ★★★★☆

Fee & Brown

50 High Street, Beckenham, BR3 1AY

Fee & Brown sets a new benchmark for coffee in London's suburbs, and has recently opened a second outlet in Orpington. Husband and wife team Ercan and Del serve a Caravan blend custom-roasted to their specifications. The artisan lunch menu, ample space, and plentiful seating make Fee & Brown an excellent choice for groups. Baked treats fill the counter top, and whole cakes are available to order. The café's dedication to quality coffee is resolutely upheld by the team of passionate young baristas.

+44(0)20 8658 1996
≥ Beckenham Junction Rail

Sister locations Orpington

MON–FRI. 7:30am – 5:00pm
SAT. 9:00am – 5:00pm
SUN. 10:00am – 4:00pm

First opened 2012
Roaster Caravan bespoke blend
Machine La Marzocco Linea, 3 groups
Grinder Mazzer Robur, Mazzer Super Jolly

Espresso £2.20
Cappuccino £2.40
Latte £2.40
Flat white £2.40

MAP REF. **114**

COFFEE
4.25 / 5

OVERALL
4.50 / 5 ★★★★✫

Four Corners Cafe

12 Lower Marsh, SE1 7RJ

Four Corners is a bright, quirky café decorated with posters bearing punchy coffee-related puns and littered with travel magazines and paraphernalia. Owner Gary Baxter's vision puts it as a crossroads, halfway between a coffee shop and hostel, a place for people who are coming, going, or just dreaming of their next big adventure. While you plan your travels, whether to Sydenham or Sydney, enjoy a coffee made with Ozone beans, pulled on a La Marzocco Linea, and a buttery, to-die-for Balthazar pastry.

+44(0)20 8617 9591
www.four-corners-cafe.com
Waterloo / Lambeth North

MON-WED. 7:30am - 5:30pm
THU-FRI. 7:30am - 6:30pm
SAT. 10:00am - 5:00pm
SUN. 10:00am - 4:00pm

First opened 2013
Roaster Ozone Coffee Roasters
Machine La Marzocco Linea, 2 groups
Grinder Mazzer Major

Espresso £2.00
Cappuccino £2.50
Latte £2.60
Flat white £2.50

MAP REF. 115

COFFEE 4.00 / 5   OVERALL 4.00 / 5 ★★★★☆

General Store

174 Bellenden Road, SE15 4BW

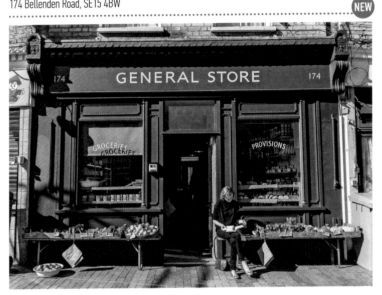

General Store is one of a rare breed of delicatessen with a real understanding of speciality coffee. Workshop espresso is pulled from a La Marzocco Linea, and an assortment of the Clerkenwell roaster's single origin beans are available whole or ground to order. The owners' passion for quality food and drink is abundantly clear in the irresistible range of provisions filling the shelves: fresh fruit, vegetables, dry goods, meats and cheeses. All produce is selected with an exceptionally keen eye for provenance and seasonality.

+44(0)20 7642 2129
www.generalsto.re
⊖ Peckham Rye

MON-TUE. Closed
WED-FRI. 9:00am - 7:00pm
SAT. 10:00am - 5:00pm
SUN. 10:00am - 4:00pm

First opened 2013
Roaster Workshop Coffee Co.
Machine La Marzocco Linea, 2 groups
Grinder Mazzer Super Jolly

Espresso £2.00
Cappuccino £2.60
Latte £2.60
Flat white £2.60

MAP REF. 116

COFFEE
4.25 / 5

OVERALL
4.25 / 5

129

Monmouth Coffee Company Borough

2 Park Street, SE1 9AB

Monmouth Coffee Company has developed a cult-like following among many Londoners who make weekly pilgrimages to this coffee mecca. The Borough Market venue, larger than the Covent Garden premises, is incredibly popular with market regulars and tourists, and is appropriately surrounded by some of the city's finest producers of foods and beverages. Fridays and Saturdays are extremely busy, so a weekday trip is a safer bet. Also worth a visit is Monmouth's Bermondsey outpost, at Arch 3 Spa North, open Saturdays only 9:00am – 1:30pm.

+44(0)20 7232 3010
www.monmouthcoffee.co.uk
⊖ London Bridge

Sister locations Covent Garden / Bermondsey

MON-SAT. 7:30am - 6:00pm
SUN. Closed

First opened 2001
Roaster Monmouth Coffee Company
Machine La Marzocco Linea, 2 groups x2
Grinder Mazzer Robur x2

Espresso £1.50
Cappuccino £2.50
Latte £2.50
Flat white £2.50

MAP REF. 117

COFFEE 4.50 / 5   OVERALL 4.50 / 5 ★★★★✦

No67 at South London Gallery

67 Peckham Road, SE5 8UH

Set within a handsome townhouse adjoining the South London Gallery, No67 is a popular café and dining room frequently packed out for weekend brunch. At less busy periods it offers a soothing respite from the din of busy Camberwell. The chocolaty Allpress coffee is handled well, and makes an excellent compliment to the outstanding Full Spanglish breakfast. Open well into the evening, No67 is also an ideal spot to enjoy cocktails and craft beer with the cultured South London crowd.

+44(0)20 7252 7649
www.number67.co.uk
⊖ Peckham Rye / Denmark Hill

MON. Closed
TUE. 8:00am - 6:30pm
WED-FRI. 8:00am - 11:00pm
SAT. 10:00am - 11:00pm
SUN. 10:00am - 6:30pm

First opened 2010
Roaster Allpress Espresso
Machine La Marzocco FB/80, 2 groups
Grinder Mazzer Robur, Mazzer Super Jolly

Espresso £1.30 / £1.80
Cappuccino £2.30 / £2.80
Latte £2.30 / £2.80
Flat white £2.30 / £2.80

MAP REF. 118

COFFEE 4.25 / 5   OVERALL 4.25 / 5 ★★★★✦

ScooterCaffè

132 Lower Marsh, SE1 7AE

The brainchild of New Zealand ex-aircraft engineer Craig O'Dwyer, ScooterCaffè started life as a Vespa workshop. However, O'Dwyer soon branched out into coffee and now his collection of vintage machinery and scooter memorabilia adorns a truly unique café space. The moody basement area hosts movie, music and comedy nights. Coffee is made on a beautiful 1960s espresso machine, accompanied by vintage grinders. ScooterCaffè is one of London's most unique retro coffee experiences.

+44(0)20 7620 1421
⊖ Lambeth North / Waterloo

Sister locations Cable Café

MON-THU. 8:30am - 11:00pm
FRI. 8:30am - 12:00am
SAT. 10:00am - 12:00am
SUN. 10:00am - 11:00pm

First opened 2009
Roaster ScooterCaffè bespoke blend
Machine 1965 Gaggia, 3 groups
Grinder Quick Mill, vintage Omer

Espresso £1.50
Cappuccino £2.20
Latte £2.20
Flat white £2.20

MAP REF. **119**

COFFEE 3.75 / 5	🫘🫘🫘🫘🫘	OVERALL 4.00 / 5	★★★★★

St. David Coffee House

5 David's Road, SE23 3EP

St. David Coffee House brims with retro charm. Local artists, actors, musicians and families come here in droves to sip espresso among the books, stacks of vinyl, and vintage movie memorabilia. The owners host regular events, such as pizza nights in collaboration with sourdough pizza purveyors Van Dough. This isn't a café which is trying hard to be liked; the atmosphere feels welcoming and uncontrived. Its easy-going nature and strong community links have made it very much part of Forest Hill life.

+44(0)20 8291 6646
www.stdavidcoffeehouse.co.uk
⊖ Forest Hill

MON. Closed
TUE-FRI. 8:00am - 6:00pm
SAT. 9:00am - 6:00pm
SUN. 10:00am - 4:00pm

First opened 2010
Roaster Square Mile Coffee Roasters and guests
Machine Rancilio Classe 10, 2 groups
Grinder Anfim

Espresso £1.50 / £1.70
Cappuccino £2.40
Latte £2.40
Flat white £2.30

MAP REF. **120**

COFFEE 4.00 / 5	🫘🫘🫘🫘🫘	OVERALL 4.00 / 5	★★★★★

Volcano Coffee House

Parkhall Trading Estate, 40 Martell Road, SE21 8EN

Volcano operates from a former electronics factory, surprisingly located among a row of terraced houses. This architecturally impressive building houses the roastery, and a spacious café. Opt for Volcano's own 'Fullsteam' espresso blend, or try a range of single estate filters. A collection of antique coffee machines and a vintage roaster displayed on gallery-style plinths announce the founders' shared love for classic machinery. Volcano resonates with a deep passion for espresso culture, past and present.

+44(0)20 8761 8415
www.volcanocoffeeworks.com
≷ West Norwood Rail / West Dulwich Rail

MON-FRI. 8:00am - 4:30pm
SAT. 9:00am - 4:30pm
SUN. Closed

First opened 2012
Roaster Volcano Coffee Works
Machine Rocket Linea Professionale, 2 groups
Grinder Mazzer Major, Mazzer Super Jolly

Espresso £2.00
Cappuccino £2.20
Latte £2.20
Flat white £2.20

MAP REF. **121**

COFFEE 4.75 / 5   OVERALL 4.50 / 5 ★★★★✬

With Jam and Bread

386 Lee High Road, SE12 8RW

Photo courtesy of the venue

With Jam and Bread is a cheerful café in which you could happily spend an entire afternoon. Passionate owner Jennie Milsom is also a food and drink writer. This child-friendly venue combines the best elements of a homely neighbourhood retreat with coffee of a standard rarely encountered in London's suburban belt. Delicious lunch and cake options are also available. Occupying the site of a former art gallery, With Jam and Bread retains an exhibition space towards the rear.

+44(0)20 8318 4040
www.withjamandbread.com
≷ Lee Rail / Hither Green Rail

MON–FRI. 8:00am - 3:00pm
SAT. 9:30am - 4:00pm
SUN. Closed

First opened 2011
Roaster Dark Fluid
Machine La Marzocco Linea, 2 groups
Grinder Anfim, Mazzer Super Jolly

Espresso £1.80
Cappuccino £2.60
Latte £2.60
Flat white £2.50

MAP REF. **122**

COFFEE 4.00 / 5 🫘 🫘 🫘 🫘 🫘

OVERALL 4.25 / 5 ★ ★ ★ ★ ☆

133

South West

South West London contains a dizzying array of cultural influences, from the Afro-Caribbean heritage of Brixton to the antipodean-influenced lifestyle of Clapham and the genteel suburban rhythms of Putney. The area's colourful and creative coffee culture reflects these unique influences and local quirks.

Artisan Putney

203 Upper Richmond Road, Putney, SW15 6SG

TOP 30

Photo courtesy of the venue

Artisan's motto "Obsessively passionate about coffee" is an apt philosophy for this busy café. Both Putney and its sister venue now benefit from advanced water filtration systems, and have added beautiful single origin coffees from Nude. The warm, light-filled space is furnished with quirky furniture, and the inventive loyalty scheme encourages customers to spin a 'wheel of fortune' to determine their reward. Everyone from mums with prams to picky coffee geeks will be met by a genuinely warm welcome and superb coffee.

+44(0)20 8617 3477
www.artisancoffee.co.uk
⊖ East Putney / ⇌ Putney Rail

Sister locations Stamford Brook

MON–FRI. 7:00am – 6:00pm
SAT. 8:00am – 6:00pm
SUN. 8:30am – 6:00pm

First opened 2011
Roaster Allpress Espresso, Nude Espresso
Machine La Marzocco FB/80, 3 groups
Grinder Mazzer Robur, Mazzer Super Jolly, Mahlkönig Tanzania

Espresso £1.50 / £1.90
Cappuccino £2.20 / £2.50
Latte £2.20 / £2.50
Flat white £2.20 / £2.50

MAP REF. **123**

COFFEE 4.50 / 5

OVERALL 4.50 / 5 ★★★★✬

Birdhouse

123 St John's Hill, SW11 1SZ

This perfectly formed café is a striking addition to St John's Hill. The interior is light, beautifully furnished in brushed steel and vintage wood, punctuated with splashes of bright yellow. Bird images and other avian touches create a unique experience, and an old carpenter's work block serves a new duty as a coffee bar. At weekends Birdhouse is a flurry of activity as plates of steaming baked eggs and beautifully-poured flat whites make their way to brunching Battersea locals.

+44(0)20 7228 6663
www.birdhou.se
⊖ Clapham Junction

MON–FRI. 7:00am – 4:00pm
SAT–SUN. 9:00am – 5:00pm

First opened 2011
Roaster Climpson & Sons
Machine La Marzocco Linea, 3 groups
Grinder Anfim, Mazzer Robur E

Espresso £2.00
Cappuccino £2.40 / £2.80
Latte £2.40 / £2.80
Flat white £2.40 / £2.80

MAP REF.

COFFEE 4.50 / 5 ●●●●◐

OVERALL 4.25 / 5 ★★★★✬

The Black Lab Coffee House

18 Clapham Common Southside, SW4 7AB

The Black Lab Coffee House is a warm and cosy choice in an area surprisingly light on good cafés. The recently refurbished venue with comfortable seating is a great place to catch up with friends, but can fill up rapidly at weekends. The Climpson & Sons roast is pulled through a new La Marzocco, and Head Barista Connor Bramley (formerly of respected Paris coffee shop Coutume Café) has furthered the attention to coffee quality. Single estate coffees brewed by AeroPress are also offered at less busy periods.

+44(0)20 7738 8441
www.blacklabcoffee.com
Clapham Common

MON-FRI. 7:30am - 5:30pm
SAT-SUN. 9:00am - 5:00pm

First opened 2010
Roaster Climpson & Sons
Machine La Marzocco Linea, 2 groups
Grinder Mahlkönig K30, Mazzer Super Jolly

Espresso £1.80
Cappuccino £2.40
Latte £2.50
Flat white £2.40

MAP REF. 125

Brew Battersea

45 Northcote Road, SW11 1NJ

A favourite with the Northcote Road set, Brew is a cheerful antidote to the many chain coffee stores nearby. Simple and cosy, Brew offers Union coffee and a comprehensive menu in a breezy, laidback environment. However, this café is best known for its sensational breakfasts, which feature only the best-quality local ingredients, as well as juices and smoothies. A tantalising dinner menu is also on offer, complemented by a beer and wine list.

+44(0)20 7585 2198
www.brew-cafe.com
Clapham Junction

Sister locations Wimbledon / Wandsworth

MON-SAT. 7:00am - 10:00pm
SUN. 7:00am - 6:00pm

First opened 2008
Roaster Union Hand-Roasted
Machine La Marzocco Linea, 2 groups
Grinder Mazzer Super Jolly

Espresso £2.30 / £2.60
Cappuccino £2.90
Latte £2.90
Flat white £2.90

MAP REF. 126

South West

138

Brickwood

16 Clapham Common South Side, SW4 7AB

NEW

Brickwood brings proper Aussie-style coffee and brunches to Clapham. Corn fritters with a choice of hallumi and poached egg, or avocado and chorizo ought to sort you out after a heavy Friday night. With an outdoor courtyard at the rear, visitors can enjoy their sunny Antipodean brunch under a (hopefully!) bright English sky. The punchy Caravan coffee perfectly compliments the food's bold flavours, and is confidently prepared by enthusiastic baristas on a stunning mint green La Marzocco, affectionately nicknamed 'Lola'.

+44(0)20 7819 9614
www.brickwoodlondon.com
⊖ Clapham Common

MON-FRI. 7:00am - 6:00pm
SAT-SUN. 9:00am - 6:00pm

First opened 2013
Roaster Caravan
Machine La Marzocco FB/80, 2 groups
Grinder Mazzer Major

Espresso £2.00
Cappuccino £2.40
Latte £2.40
Flat white £2.30

MAP REF. **127**

COFFEE 4.25 / 5   OVERALL 4.25 / 5 ★★★★⯨

Federation Coffee

Unit 77-78 Brixton Village Market, Coldharbour Lane, SW9 8PS

Federation has led a flourishing of foodie culture in the rapidly gentrifying Brixton Village Market, and is now surrounded by a host of other cafés and restaurants following its lead. Federation's roasting operation has ceased for the time being, but the coffee – supplied by acclaimed South London roasters Alchemy – is worth making a special trip for. The seating arrayed around the outside of the café affords a prime position to people-watch and soak up the lively atmosphere of the covered market.

www.federationcoffee.com
⊖ Brixton

Sister locations Brighton Terrace Takeaway Hatch

MON-FRI. 8:00am - 5:00pm
SAT. 9:00am - 6:00pm
SUN. 9:00am - 5:00pm

First opened 2010
Roaster Alchemy
Machine Synesso Cyncra, 3 groups
Grinder Mazzer Robur, Anfim

Espresso £2.00
Cappuccino £2.60
Latte £2.60
Flat white £2.60

MAP REF. **128**

COFFEE 4.50 / 5   OVERALL 4.50 / 5 ★★★★⯨

Grind Coffee Bar Putney

79 Lower Richmond Road, SW15 1ET

This stylish, contemporary café was one of the pioneers on the now-thriving Putney coffee scene. Grind's friendly antipodean atmosphere and excellent flat whites make it popular with local ex-pats, but its bespoke house blend from London Coffee Roasters and use of British ingredients give it a decidedly local outlook. The café's corner location and tempting range of homemade cakes and savouries make it difficult to pass without popping in for a coffee and a chat with the genial team of baristas.

+44(0)20 8789 5101
www.grindcoffeebar.co.uk
⊖ Putney Bridge

Sister locations Westfield Stratford City

MON-THU. 7:00am - 6:00pm
FRI. 7:00am - 9:00pm
SAT. 8:00am - 9:00pm
SUN. 8:00am - 6:00pm

First opened 2010
Roaster London Coffee Roasters
Machine La Marzocco Strada EP, 2 groups
Grinder Mazzer Robur x2

Espresso £1.80
Cappuccino £2.30 / £2.70
Latte £2.30 / £2.70
Flat white £2.30 / £2.70

MAP REF. **129**

COFFEE 4.50 / 5   OVERALL 4.25 / 5 ★★★★⯨

The Lido Cafe

Brockwell Lido, Dulwich Road, SE24 0PA

A bracing dip in Brockwell Lido is guaranteed to wake you up in the morning (just as effectively as a double espresso!) Thankfully, you don't need to take the plunge to enjoy the hospitality at The Lido Cafe. In summer, the palm-shaded terrace overlooking the pool is a special spot to sip flat whites, or even indulge in a Prosecco brunch. Open for breakfast, lunch or dinner all year round, this Art Deco retreat is a truly unique addition to London's café culture.

+44(0)20 7737 8183
www.thelidocafe.co.uk
⇌ Herne Hill Rail

MON-TUE. 9:00am - 5:00pm
WED-SAT. 9:00am - 11:00pm
SUN. 9:00am - 5:00pm

First opened 2009
Roaster Allpress Espresso
Machine La Marzocco FB/80, 3 groups
Grinder Mazzer Robur

Espresso £1.90
Cappuccino £2.50
Latte £2.50
Flat white £2.40

MAP REF. **130**

COFFEE 4.25 / 5	OVERALL 4.25 / 5

M1lk

20 Bedford Hill, SW12 9RG

Photo courtesy of the venue

M1lk is a magnificent medley of artisan coffee and Aussie-style food, with a sprinkling of British eccentricity. The playful and nostalgic theme borders on the bizarre with the café's baby head motif. The hip team take their espresso very seriously, squeezing every drop of performance from their La Marzocco Linea. Alternatively, try an AeroPress to appreciate the subtleties of the single origins on offer. Cupping classes are also available for those interested in developing their own coffee expertise.

+44(0)20 8772 9085
www.m1lk.co.uk
⊖ Balham

MON–SAT. 8:00am – 5:00pm
SUN. 9:00am – 5:00pm

First opened 2012
Roaster Workshop Coffee Co.
Machine La Marzocco Linea, 2 groups
Grinder Anfim, Mazzer Robur E, Mahlkönig EK 43

Espresso £2.00
Cappuccino £2.40
Latte £2.50
Flat white £2.40

MAP REF. 131

COFFEE 4.50 / 5 **OVERALL** 4.25 / 5 ★★★★☆

Tried & True

279 Upper Richmond Road, SW15 6SP

Tried & True brings the best of Kiwi café culture to suburban Putney. The vibe is relaxed and welcoming. The interior eschews voguish shabby chic in favour of a bright, clean and refreshingly modern aesthetic. The baristas pull shots with utmost care, constantly re-calibrating the equipment to keep the Square Mile coffee spot on. A beautiful garden beckons in the summer months, and the delectable brunch menu has few rivals. Tried & True is one of a rare breed of top-class neighbourhood cafés.

+44(0)20 8789 0410
www.triedandtruecafe.co.uk
⊖ Putney

MON-FRI. 8:00am - 4:00pm
SAT-SUN. 8:30am - 4:30pm

First opened 2012
Roaster Square Mile Coffee Roasters
Machine La Marzocco FB/80, 3 groups
Grinder Mazzer Robur E, Mazzer Super Jolly

Espresso £2.20
Cappuccino £2.60
Latte £2.80
Flat white £2.60

MAP REF. **132**

COFFEE
4.25 / 5

OVERALL
4.25 / 5

West

Home to some of London's wealthiest residents, world-renowned museums and lavish department stores, West London has a well established café culture. The number of quality-focussed coffee bars has grown in recent months, but still has a long way to go to match other London neighbourhoods.

Artisan Stamford Brook

372 King Street, W6 0RX

West

Photo courtesy of the venue

Owners Edwin and Magda's passion for coffee began with a trip to origin, where they contributed to development work with coffee farmers. Artisan's London cafés do justice to the work of growers and roasters by diligently extracting every last drop of goodness. The interior's electric blue walls contrast magnificently with the copper counter and stools, creating a striking environment in which to enjoy the finished product. Upholding their reputation for coffee excellence, the team now run coffee brewing masterclasses for customers.

+44(0)20 3302 1434
www.artisancoffee.co.uk
⊖ Stamford Brook

Sister locations Putney

MON-FRI. 7:30am – 6:00pm
SAT-SUN. 8:30am – 6:00pm

First opened 2013
Roaster Allpress Espresso, Nude Espresso
Machine La Marzocco FB/80, 3 groups
Grinder Mazzer Robur, Mazzer Super Jolly, Mahlkönig Tanzania

Espresso £1.50 / £1.90
Cappuccino £2.20 / £2.50
Latte £2.20 / £2.50
Flat white £2.20 / £2.50

MAP REF. **133**

COFFEE 4.50 / 5

OVERALL 4.50 / 5 ★★★★⯪

Electric Coffee Co.

40 Haven Green, Ealing, W5 2NX

Stepping inside this Ealing enclave, one's gaze is immediately stolen by the Kees van der Westen Mirage coffee machine. Crafted with aircraft-grade aluminium, this stunning machine is the supercharged dynamo of Electric Coffee Co. Piloted by an enthusiastic team, the Mirage fires out gutsy espresso custom-roasted by Volcano Coffee Works. Filter coffee is also available should you prefer a more gentle take-off. Electric Coffee Co. is one of the best third wave coffee shops in the west.

+44(0)20 8991 1010
www.electriccoffee.co.uk
⊖ Ealing Broadway

MON-FRI. 7:00am - 6:00pm
SAT-SUN. 8:00am - 6:00pm

First opened 2008
Roaster Square Mile Coffee Roasters, Volcano Coffee Works bespoke blend
Machine Kees van der Westen Mirage Veloce, 3 groups
Grinder Mazzer Robur E x2, Anfim Super Caimano

Espresso £1.90
Cappuccino £2.40 / £2.60
Latte £2.40 / £2.60
Flat white £2.40

MAP REF. ●134

COFFEE 4.50 / 5   OVERALL 4.50 / 5 ★★★★✬

Fernandez & Wells South Kensington

8a Exhibition Road , W7 2HF

Fernandez & Wells' newest venue is a godsend for coffee-starved West Londoners and visitors to the nearby museums. The interior's high ceiling and elegant cornicing resonate with South Kensington's noble architecture. Cured meats hang artfully against the rear wall, accompanied by a shelf of well-chosen wines. There's plenty of seating round the back, which is fortunate as you'll almost certainly want to complement your Has Bean coffee with a plate of charcuterie.

+44(0)20 7589 7473
www.fernandezandwells.com
⊖ South Kensington

Sister locations Somerset House / Beak Street / Lexington Street

MON–FRI. 8:00am – 10:00pm
SAT. 9:00am – 10:00pm
SUN. 9:00am – 8:00pm

First opened 2012
Roaster Has Bean bespoke blend
Machine Synesso Cyncra, 3 groups
Grinder Mazzer Robur E x2, Mahlkönig Tanzania

Espresso £2.40
Cappuccino £2.80
Latte £2.80
Flat white £2.80

MAP REF. **135**

COFFEE 4.50 / 5

OVERALL 4.50 / 5 ★★★★⯪

Hally's

60 New Kings Road, SW6 4LS

NEW

The vibe at Hally's is airy California cool. The reclaimed clapboard and whitewashed brick walls are punctuated by citrus yellow bar stools and neon signs. You may just be popping in for a Monmouth coffee, but be prepared to stay for longer once you catch sight of the food on offer, which includes an outstanding array of salads and a bold-flavoured brunch menu. Hally's is a superb neighbourhood café for the well-heeled Fulham faithful.

+44(0)20 3302 7408
www.hallysparsonsgreen.com
⊖ Parsons Green

MON-SUN. 8:00am - 6:00pm

First opened 2013
Roaster Monmouth Coffee Company
Machine La Marzocco Linea, 3 groups
Grinder Obel

Espresso £2.00
Cappuccino £2.50
Latte £2.50
Flat white £2.50

MAP REF. 136

COFFEE 4.00 / 5	OVERALL 4.25 / 5

Talkhouse Coffee

275 Portobello Road, W11 1LR

Photo courtesy of the venue

The minimalist decor, whitewashed walls and high ceilings lend Talkhouse a sense of calming gravitas. This impressive space near the vibrant Portobello market has rapidly established its third wave coffee credentials, employing some of London's most talented baristas and offering beans from top artisan roasters. Overseen by Latte Art Champion Miguel Lamora, the coffee is meticulously prepared and presented. When it comes to a quality brew in west London, Talkhouse is the name on everyone's lips.

+44(0)20 7221 8992
www.talkhousecoffee.com
⊖ Ladbroke Grove

MON-FRI. 8:00am - 5:00pm
SAT. 9:30am - 7:00pm
SUN. 9:30 - 5:00pm

First opened 2013
Roaster Workshop Coffee Co., Square Mile Coffee Roasters, James Gourmet
Machine Synesso Hydra, 3 groups
Grinder Anfim, Mahlkönig Tanzania

Espresso £2.20
Cappuccino £3.00
Flat white £2.70

MAP REF. 137

COFFEE 4.75 / 5 🫘🫘🫘🫘🫘

OVERALL 4.50 / 5 ★★★★✬

Tomtom Coffee House

114 Ebury Street, SW1W 9QD

Set in leafy Belgravia, Tomtom Coffee House is a neighbourhood favourite with an upmarket feel. A large round table and abundance of natural light fosters a friendly and communal atmosphere, making this a perfect choice for a lazy afternoon coffee hangout with friends. Tomtom's coffee is custom roasted by Dorset's Reads Coffee, and is available for customers to purchase in whole bean form. Sister shop Tomtom Cigars is conveniently located across the road on Elizabeth Street.

+44(0)20 7730 1771
www.tomtom.co.uk
⊖ Victoria / Sloane Square

Winter:
MON-FRI. 8:00am - 5:00pm
SAT-SUN. 9:00am - 5:00pm
Summer:
MON-TUE. 8:00am - 6:00pm
WED-FRI. 8:00am - 9:00pm
SAT. 9:00am - 9:00pm
SUN. 9:00am - 6:00pm

First opened 2008
Roaster Reads Coffee bespoke blend
Machine La Marzocco Linea, 2 groups
Grinder Ceado E92, Mahlkönig Guatemala

Espresso £1.80
Cappuccino £2.60
Latte £2.60
Flat white £2.90

MAP REF. 138

COFFEE 4.00 / 5

OVERALL 4.00 / 5 ★★★★☆

Coffee Knowledge

Behind every cup of coffee is a unique story. On its journey from coffee tree to cup, coffee passes through the hands of a number of skilled individuals. Over the following pages, expert contributors share their specialist knowledge. As you will see, the coffee we enjoy is the result of a rich and complex process, and there is always something new to learn.

Coffee at Origin

by **Mike Riley**, Falcon Speciality Green Coffee Importers

If you go into London's vibrant coffee community today and ask any good barista what makes a perfect cup of coffee, they will always tell you that it starts with the bean. Beyond the roasting technique, the perfect grind, and exact temperatures and precision pressure of a modern espresso machine, we must look to the dedicated coffee farmer who toils away in the tropical lands of Africa, Asia and Latin America. They are the first heroes of our trade.

Approximately 25 million people in over 50 countries are involved in producing coffee. The bean, or seed to be exact, is extracted from cherries that most commonly ripen red but sometimes orange or yellow. The cherries are usually hand-picked then processed by various means. Sometimes they are dried in the fruit under tropical sunshine until they resemble raisins – a process known as 'natural'. The 'honey process' involves pulping the fresh cherries to extract the beans which are then sundried, still coated in their sticky mucilage. Alternatively, in the 'washed process', the freshly pulped beans are left to stand in tanks of water for several hours where enzyme activity breaks down the mucilage, before they are sundried on concrete patios or raised beds. Each method has a profound impact on the ultimate flavour of the coffee.

The term 'speciality coffee' is used to differentiate the world's best from the rest. This means it has to be Arabica, the species of coffee that is often bestowed with incredible flavours - unlike its hardy cousin Robusta which is usually reserved for commercial products and many instant blends. But being Arabica alone is by no means enough for a coffee to achieve the speciality tag, since the best beans are usually those grown at higher altitude on rich and fertile soils. As well as country and region of origin, the variety is important too; Bourbon, Typica, Caturra, Catuai, Pacamara and Geisha to name but a few. Just as Shiraz and Chardonnay grapes have their own complex flavours, the same is true of coffee's varieties. Some of the world's most amazing coffees are the result of the farmer's innovative approach to experimentation with growing and production techniques, meaning that today's speciality roaster is able to source coffees of incredible complexity and variation.

A good coffee establishment will showcase coffees when they are at their best – freshly harvested and seasonal, just like good fruit and vegetables. Seasonal espresso blends change throughout the year to reflect this.

As speciality coffee importers we source stand-out coffees by regularly travelling to origin countries. Direct trade with farmers is always our aim. Above all, we pay sustainable prices and encourage them to treat their land, and those who work it, with respect. Such an approach is increasingly demanded by London's speciality coffee community in order to safeguard the industry's future.

Photo: Alessandro Bonuzzi

Small Batch Roasting

by **Kurt Stewart**, Roaster and Co-owner, Volcano Coffee Works

I was brought up in a household dedicated to pickling, baking, sauce making and preserving. After experimenting with home brewing and wine making, my first foray into the aromatic world of small batch roasting was inevitable.

My own first experiments in small batch roasting started at home with some green beans and a wok. Of course roasting at home is much like home cooking, but when the term is applied to a commercial enterprise, it encompasses the passion and adventure of a home cook with the control and precision of a gourmet chef.

The art behind developing and building a roasting profile for a particular coffee is approached in the same way a chef develops cuisine, or a vintner crafts a wine. Culinary rules and science apply in equal measure. The roaster builds layers of flavour, working with the ingredients, sometimes pushing or manipulating the properties of an individual bean, to achieve the desired balance of sweetness, acidity, body, and the right mouth-feel and aftertaste. Coffee and wine share a vocabulary of descriptors, but as coffee has more flavour molecules than wine, coffee descriptors reach further into the culinary world. You will hear words describing aspects of flavour and taste senses, such as fruit acidity, sweet roundness, viscous syrup body, juicy plum, creamy, buttery, velvet chocolate textures. Delicious!

When a green bean is roasted, three fundamental processes occur that impact the flavours of the bean: enzyme by-products develop (giving the floral, citrus and fruity aromas), sugars brown (giving the sweet, caramel and nutty aromas), and plant fibres in the bean are roasted, known as dry-distillation (giving the spicy and smokey flavours). Only the enzyme by-products (which come from the coffee plant itself) are due to the bean chosen for roasting, whilst the remaining two processes are the result of how the bean is roasted. This is why no two small batch roasters will create an identical flavour profile from the same bean. Like chefs, each roaster will identify with, single out and highlight a flavour or combination of flavours which pleases, satisfies or amazes their palate.

Small Batch Roasting is a term reserved for those using roasting equipment controlled by the human hand rather than computers. A skilled roaster who understands his equipment, maintains ducting, understands heat/air ratios and extraction principles, coupled with following some basic fundamentals, can draw out origin characteristics and individual nuances, and create a roast where the optimum flavour potential is realised.

The roasting equipment itself is fundamentally a steel drum, which is usually heated by a gas flame. The drum constantly revolves, and at around 10 minutes of roasting at 203-205°C the developing beans reach 'first crack' (a bit like popcorn cracking). If roasting stops here, it will be a mild or lighter roast. When roasting continues, samples are taken with every revolution of the drum and the roaster observes the developing bean's colour, mass and aroma. The roaster may apply more or less heat or air and will remove the beans once they have reached the desired roast profile. This is usually within a 20 minute roasting time and often before second crack is reached as beyond this point the beans can lose their subtle origin characteristics and begin to take on a generic burnt flavour. The beans then enter the cooling tray until cool to touch. This process is in stark contrast to the large scale computer controlled commercial roasting process that takes between 90 seconds and 10 minutes at temperatures in excess of 360°C. The beans are then doused with water to cool them. Although this is the most economic way to roast beans, it takes away any

input by the roaster and does not give the bean enough time to develop fully.

When a roastery operation gets to such a scale that the roaster becomes distanced from their beans due to mechanised roasting processes and machinery, the instinct and hands-on effect that define a small batch roaster's product will always become somewhat diminished. And therein lies the excitement and diversity that small batch roasting offers over and above large-scale operations. It comes down to the physical ability of a talented roaster to exercise his or her senses, passion, enthusiasm, and the art of roasting.

Coffee Tasting

by **Lynsey Harley**, Coffee Specialist and Q Grader, Falcon Speciality Green Coffee Importers

Coffee tasting is the process of identifying the characteristics of a particular coffee. In the coffee industry, professional 'cupping' sessions are conducted to evaluate coffees on a range of attributes. Cupping helps coffee buyers select which coffees to buy, and identify desirable attributes for formulating blends.

Coffee is most commonly scored using The Specialty Coffee Association of America (SCAA) system. Coffees achieving a score of 85 or higher (from a maximum of 100) are regarded as 'specialty' grade. These coffees have no defects and have a very distinct pleasant flavour profile. Coffees are scored on the following attributes: aroma, flavour, aftertaste, acidity, body, sweetness, cleanliness, uniformity and balance.

The cupping process follows a set procedure: 8.25g of coarsely ground coffee is measured into a shallow cup, specifically designed for the purpose. 150ml of water heated to 92°C is added and left for 4 minutes. Next, a spoon is used to break and remove the 'crust', which provides the first opportunity to sample the coffee's aroma. After a further 6 minutes, the cupper begins to taste the coffee. Different attributes are evaluated at intervals as the coffee cools.

70°C: Flavour and Aftertaste

Flavour: The coffee's principle flavour; what are your taste buds telling you?

Aftertaste: The length of positive flavour qualities after the coffee has been swallowed.

70°C – 60°C: Acidity and Body

Acidity: Bright for positive acidity, sour for negative. Positive acidity adds to the coffee's sweetness.

Body: The 'weight' of the brew. Is it heavy like a good red wine, or light and refined like a sauvignon blanc?

38°C: Sweetness and Cleanliness.

Sweetness: Is the coffee sweet and pleasing?

Cleanliness: When no defects are found, the cup is clean.

Balance: Greater than the sum of its parts. Flavour, aftertaste, acidity and body work together to achieve balance.

One coffee can taste dramatically different depending on the processing method. Washing coffees increases the acidity, whilst the semi-washed process gives a honeyed sweetness to the coffee. The natural processing method can increase the sweetness, and can also encourage development of more obscure flavours including strawberry, blueberry and creamy notes.

Tasting coffee at home can be fun; exploring what a coffee can offer in terms of flavour, sweetness and other attributes is exciting. Your local speciality coffee shop can offer advice on which coffees are in season, and many will sell beans for you to experiment with at home. There's a coffee out there for everyone.

SCAA Coffee taster's wheel

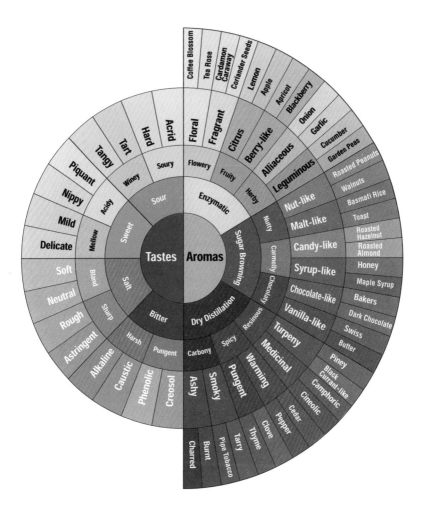

159

Coffee Grinding

by **Jeremy Challender**, Co-owner and Director of Training, Prufrock Coffee and the

Grinder technology is about to change radically. Machine design, techniques behind the bar and hand brewing methodology have improved rapidly over recent years. Manufacturers are starting to address this by seeking feedback from users as well as lab testing. Home users can benefit from these changes too. New designs entering the market have drawn directly from the experiences of barista champions. Grinder designers are seeking professional and consumer feedback on taste, flavour and ergonomics through direct collaboration and field testing. Manufacturers are aware that we need development to continue and, now more than ever, baristas have a voice in this process. To be a barista in this time of grinder development is very exciting.

With all brew methods the challenge is replicating flavour and strength. Once we've got a precise brew recipe for a coffee we stand a better chance of extracting our coffee consistently. Commercially, the easiest way to navigate from this baseline towards the optimum extraction level is with micro-adjustments in the exposed surface area of the grinds – so the grinder is key to managing flavour in the cup.

The challenge grinder designers face is how to create consistency of grind size and shape. If you get out the microscope, and a set of test sieves, you start to realise all your grinds aren't the same size, nor are they all the same shape. If they were all the same size and shape, brewing would be much easier to control. In espresso you will have seen tiny granules

in your cup that are smaller than the holes in the filter basket. We call these fines. These small particles have very high surface area and extract very quickly. As a home brewer, you could consider following the example of many championship baristas; invest in laboratory test sieves to remove a portion of particles under a certain size to reduce over-extracted flavours.

There is a portion of particles that fit side-on between the burrs and are planed rather than ground. We call these larger particles boulders. They have a much lower surface area relative to their size and in a 30 second espresso extraction will under-extract. Wobbly hand grinders are real offenders in the production of boulders. These too can be sieved out.

Sharp burrs are considered to reduce fines production. Ceramic burrs, which many hand grinders are fitted with, are very durable but are often not very sharp to start with. The material of choice at the moment is titanium-coated steel. Large burr diameter is linked to lower production of fines and boulders (more 'modal' distribution) so enormous bag grinders are being examined for application in espresso making. Cutting systems like spice grinders produce a very high proportion of fines and boulders, so are not recommended.

Keeping the coffee cool during grinding is a challenge. Burrs get hot in use because of friction, and some of the most exciting developments recently have focused on temperature stability of the burrs and burr casing with the addition of heating elements and fans. A warm grinder behaves differently to a cold or a hot one, so the particle shape and size are dependent on both grind setting and temperature.

Modern grinder design is very focussed on ease of access for regular cleaning. Arabica coffee has up to 17% fat content. We only extract a small percentage of this into a beverage but even after a day of commercial use, a grinder will have a slick of fats and tiny fine particles built up around the burr casing and the barrel and throat of the grinder. Oils oxidise, so grinders must be opened up and thoroughly swept out on a regular basis. Burrs can be washed in soapy water or coffee cleaner, or abrasive oil absorbing grinder cleaning granules can be used. Home baristas have an advantage here by being able to clean after a few shots rather than after a full day's usage.

The final hurdle to overcome is grind retention: many grinders on the market have large barrels and throats that can store as much as 40g of grinds that must be squeezed out before fresh grinds appear. At Prufrock, we are moving away from grinders with a high retention of grinds as we are looking to optimise freshness. When grind changes are required we want the benefit of micro-adjustment to be immediate. Here, home baristas are also well placed, as hand grinders have zero retention of grinds and some very high quality espresso hand grinders are now available on the market.

Over the last decade we have felt that machine technology has been in advance of grinders. We often comment that a barista's top priority should be the choice of grinder. Find a great grinding solution and great coffee will follow.

Photo: Jacob Thue

Water - The Enigma

by **Maxwell Colonna-Dashwood**, Co-owner, Colonna and Small's, UK Barista Champion 2012

This vital ingredient is the foundation of every cup of coffee you have ever tasted, apart from the bean itself of course.

It's not just coffee that relies so dramatically on this everyday and seemingly straightforward substance. The worlds of craft beer and whisky are suitable comparisons, with breweries and distilleries proudly signifying the provenance of their water as being a vital part of their product.

A roaster, though, sells coffee, the water bit comes post sale. The water will be different and unique based on the locality of brewing, and this is on top of all of the other variables that define coffee brewing such as grinding, temperature and brew ratios. The reality is that the impact of water is rarely directly witnessed, with the other variables often being seen as the cause for dramatic flavour changes. You may be wondering right now, how big an impact can it really have?

I'm yet to present the same coffee brewed with different waters to drinkers and not have them exclaim "I can't believe how different they are, they taste like different coffees'. These aren't "coffee people" either, but customers who contested prior to the tasting that "you may be able to taste the difference but I doubt I can tell."

It may make you question whether the coffee that you tried and weren't particularly keen on, was a representative version of what the bean actually tastes like, or at the least what it is capable of tasting of like.

So, why the big difference, what is in the water?

Nearly all water that trickles out of a tap or sits in a bottle is not just water. As well as the H2O there are other bits and bobs in the water. Minerals mainly. These have a big impact not only on what we extract from the coffee but also how that flavour sits in the cup of coffee.

It's fair to say that currently the way the coffee industry discusses water is through the use of a measurement called Total Dissolved Solids (TDS).

TDS has become the measurement which is relied upon to distinguish and inform us about how water will affect our coffee. It gives us a total of everything in the water. The problem though, is that TDS doesn't tell us everything we need to know about the water; it doesn't tell us about what those solids are. On top of this, TDS meters don't measure some non-solids that have a huge impact on flavour.

In the water, we need the minerals calcium and magnesium to help pull out a lot of the desirable flavour in the coffee, but we also need the right amount of buffering ability in the water to balance the acids. This buffering ability can be noted as the bicarbonate content of the water. So for example an "empty" soft water with no minerals will lack flavour complexity and the lack of buffer will mean a more vinegary acidity.

A good test is to make the same coffee with both Evian and Tesco Ashbeck water. Evian has a good amount of calcium and magnesium to pull flavour out, but this is accompanied by a high bicarbonate content which flattens everything out and results in a heavy, bitter and chalky brew. The Ashbeck has little extraction power so is quite empty but has a low buffer so the acidity verges on sour. For bottled waters, Waitrose Essential yields pleasant results.

However the coffee shops in this guide will most likely have a trick up their sleeve. The industry filtration systems that have been developed primarily to stop scale build up in the striking and valuable espresso machines, also produce water compositions that are more often than not preferable for coffee brewing. Speciality coffee shops require all manner of specifics to be obsessed over and carefully executed. That cup of coffee that hits you and stops you in your step with intense, balanced and complex flavour will owe its brilliance to careful brewing, a knowledgeable brewer and superb equipment. However, it also owes a significant part of its beautiful character and flavour to the water it is brewed with.

Brewing Filter Coffee at Home

by **Christian Baker, David Robson & Sam Mason**, Association Coffee

Y ou may be surprised to know that filter coffee brewed at home can rival that of your favourite coffee shop. All you need is good quality ingredients and some inexpensive equipment. Keep in mind that small variations in grind coarseness, coffee / water ratio and brew time will make a significant difference to flavour, and that trial and error is the key to unlocking perfection.

Whole Beans: Whole bean coffee is superior to pre-ground. Coffee rapidly deteriorates once ground, so buy your coffee in whole bean form and store it in an air-tight container at room temperature. It should be consumed between three and thirty days after roast and ground only moments before brewing.

Water: Water is important because it makes up over 98% of the finished drink. Only use bottled water, preferably with a dry residue between 80-150mg/l. London tap water is not suitable for brewing - it will inhibit your ability to extract flavour and reveal only a fraction of a coffee's potential.

Digital scales: Get a set of scales accurate to 1g and large enough to hold your coffee brewer. Coffee is commonly measured in 'scoops' or 'tablespoons', but coffee and water are best measured by weight for greater accuracy and to ensure repeatability. Small changes in the ratio of coffee to water can have a significant impact on flavour. A good starting point is 60-70g of coffee per litre of water. Apply this ratio to meet the size of your brewer.

Grinder

A burr grinder is essential. Burr grinders are superior to blade grinders because they allow the grind coarseness to be set and produce a more consistent size of coffee fragment (critical for an even extraction). As a general rule, the coarser the grind the longer the brew time required, and vice versa. For example, an espresso needs a very fine grind whereas a French Press works with a coarser grind.

French Press

Preheat the French Press with hot water, and discard. Add 34g of coarsely ground coffee and pour in 500g of water just below boiling point (94/95°C). Steep for 4 to 5 minutes then gently plunge to the bottom. Decant the coffee straight away to avoid over-brewing (known as over-extraction).

AeroPress

The AeroPress is wonderfully versatile. It can be used with finely ground coffee and a short steep time, or with a coarser grind and a longer steep time. The latter is our preferred method for its flavour and repeatability. Preheat the AeroPress using hot water, and discard. Rinse the paper filter before securing, and place the AeroPress over a sturdy cup or jug. Add 16g of coffee and pour in 240g of water at 95°C. Secure the plunger on top, creating a seal. Steep for 3 minutes then plunge over 20 seconds.

Pour Over

We recommend using a pouring kettle for better pouring control. Place a filter paper in the cone and rinse through with hot water. Add 15g of coffee and slowly pour 30g of 95°C water to pre-soak the coffee grounds. This creates the 'bloom'. After 30 seconds add 250g of water, pouring steadily in a circular motion over the centre. It should take 1 minute and 45 seconds to pour and between 30-45 seconds to drain through. The key is to keep the flow of water steady. If the water drains too quickly/slowly, adjust the coarseness of the grind to compensate.

Stovetop

A stovetop will not make an espresso, it will, however, make a strong coffee. Pour hot water in to the base to the fill-line or just below the pressure release valve. Fill the basket with ground coffee of medium coarseness (between Pour Over and French Press). Traditional wisdom suggests a fine grind in pursuit of espresso, but stovetops extract differently to espresso machines and grinding fine is a recipe for bitter, over-extracted coffee. Screw the base to the top and place on the heat. When you hear bubbling, remove immediately and decant to ensure the brewing has stopped.

Illustrations: Zoë Barker

The**Coffee ArtProject**

Share your passion for coffee and art

Submissions invited

www.coffeeartproject.com

@TheCoffeeArtPro

Coffee Glossary

Acidity: the pleasant tartness of a coffee. Examples of acidity descriptors include lively and flat. One of the principal attributes evaluated by professional tasters when determining the quality of a coffee.

AeroPress: a hand-powered coffee brewer marketed by Aerobie Inc., and launched in 2005. Consists of two cylinders, one sliding within the other, somewhat resembling a large syringe. Water is forced through ground coffee held in place by a paper filter, creating a concentrated filter brew.

Affogato: one or more scoops of vanilla ice cream topped with a shot of espresso, served as a dessert.

Americano, Caffè Americano: a long coffee consisting of espresso with hot water added on top. Originates from the style of coffee favoured by American GIs stationed in Europe during WWII.

Arabica, Coffea arabica: the earliest cultivated species of coffee tree and the most widely grown, Arabica accounts for approximately 70% of the world's coffee. Superior in quality to Robusta, it is more delicate and is generally grown at higher altitudes.

Aroma: the fragrance produced by brewed coffee. Examples of aroma descriptors include earthy, spicy and floral. One of the principal attributes evaluated by professional tasters when determining the quality of a coffee.

Barista: a professional person skilled in making coffee, particularly one working at an espresso bar.

Blend: a combination of coffees from different countries or regions. Mixed together, they achieve a balanced flavour profile no single coffee can offer alone.

Body: describes the heaviness, thickness or relative weight of coffee on the tongue. One of the principal attributes evaluated by professional tasters when determining the quality of a coffee.

Bottomless portafilter, naked portafilter: a portafilter without spouts, allowing espresso to flow directly from the bottom of the filter basket into the cup. Allows the extraction to be monitored visually.

Brew group: the assembly protruding from the front of an espresso machine consisting of the grouphead, portafilter and basket. The brew group must be heated to a sufficient temperature to produce a good espresso.

Brew pressure: pressure of 9 bar is required for espresso extraction.

Brew temperature: the water temperature at the point of contact with coffee. Optimum brew temperature varies by extraction method. Espresso brew temperature is typically 90-95°C. A stable brew temperature is crucial for good espresso.

Brew time, extraction time: the contact time between water and coffee. Espresso brew time is typically 25-30 seconds. Brew times are dictated by a variety of factors including the grind coarseness and degree of roast.

Burr set: an integral part of a coffee grinder. Consists of a pair of rotating steel discs between which coffee beans are ground. Burrs are either flat or conical in shape.

Café con leche: a traditional Spanish coffee consisting of espresso topped with scalded milk.

Caffeine: an odourless, slightly bitter alkaloid responsible for the stimulating effect of coffee.

Cappuccino: a classic Italian coffee comprising one-third espresso, one-third steamed milk and one-third frothed milk. Traditionally 4.5oz, but in the UK usually larger. Sometimes topped with powdered chocolate or cinnamon.

Capsule: a self-contained, pre-ground, pre-pressed portion of coffee, individually sealed inside a plastic capsule. Capsule brewing systems are commonly found in domestic coffee machines. Often compatible only with certain equipment brands.

Chemex: A type of pour over coffee brewer with a distinctive hourglass-shaped vessel. Invented in 1941, the Chemex has become regarded as a design classic and is on permanent display at the Museum of Modern Art in New York City.

Cherry: the fruit of the coffee plant. Each cherry contains two coffee seeds (beans).

Cortado: a traditional short Spanish coffee consisting of espresso cut with a small quantity of steamed milk. Similar to an Italian piccolo.

Crema: the dense caramel-coloured layer that forms on the surface of an espresso. Consists of emulsified oils created by the dispersion of gases in liquid at high pressure. The presence of crema is commonly equated with a good espresso.

Cupping: a method by which professional tasters perform sensory evaluation of coffee. Hot water is poured over ground coffee and left to extract. The taster first samples the aroma, then tastes the coffee by slurping it from a spoon.

Decaffeinated: coffee with approximately 97% or more of its naturally occurring caffeine removed is classified as decaffeinated.

Dispersion screen, shower screen: a component of the grouphead that ensures even distribution of brewing water over the coffee bed in the filter basket.

Dosage: the mass of ground coffee used for a given brewing method. Espresso dosage is typically 7-10g of ground coffee (14-20g for a double).

Double espresso, doppio: typically 30-50ml extracted from 14-20g of ground coffee. The majority of coffee venues in this guide serve double shots as standard.

Drip method: a brewing method that allows brew water to seep through a bed of ground coffee by gravity, not pressure.

Espresso: the short, strong shot of coffee that forms the basis for many other coffee beverages. Made by forcing hot water at high pressure through a compressed bed of finely ground coffee.

Espresso machine: in a typical configuration, a pump delivers hot water from a boiler to the brew group, where it is forced under pressure through ground coffee held in the portafilter. A separate boiler delivers steam for milk foaming.

Extraction: the process of infusing coffee with hot water to release flavour, accomplished either by allowing ground coffee to sit in hot water for a period of time or by forcing hot water through ground coffee under pressure.

Filter method: any brewing method in which water filters through a bed of ground coffee.

Coffee Glossary contd.

Most commonly used to describe drip method brewers that use a paper filter to separate grounds from brewed coffee.

Flat white: an espresso-based beverage first made popular in Australia and New Zealand. Made with a double shot of espresso with finely steamed milk and a thin layer of microfoam. Typically served as a 5-6oz drink with latte art.

Flavour: the way a coffee tastes. Flavour descriptors include nutty and earthy. One of the principal attributes evaluated by professional tasters when determining the quality of a coffee.

French press, plunger pot, cafetiere: a brewing method that separates grounds from brewed coffee by pressing them to the bottom of the brewing receptacle with a mesh filter attached to a plunger.

Froth, foam: created when milk is heated and aerated, usually with hot steam from an espresso machine's steam wand. Used to create a traditional cappuccino.

Green coffee, green beans: unroasted coffee. The dried seeds from the coffee cherry.

Grind: the degree of coarseness to which coffee beans are ground. A crucial factor in determining the nature of a coffee brew. Grind coarseness should be varied in accordance with the brewing method. Methods involving longer brew times call for a coarse grind. A fine grind is required for brew methods with a short extraction time such as espresso.

Grinder: a vital piece of equipment for making coffee. Coffee beans must be ground evenly for a good extraction. Most commonly motorised, but occasionally manual. Burr grinders are the best choice for an even grind.

Group: see Brew Group

Grouphead: a component of the brew group containing the locking connector for the portafilter and the dispersion screen.

Honey process, pulped natural, semi-washed: a method of processing coffee where the cherry is removed (pulped), but the beans are sun-dried with mucilage intact. Typically results in a sweet flavour profile with a balanced acidity.

Latte, caffè latte: an Italian beverage made with espresso combined with steamed milk, traditionally topped with foamed milk and served in a glass. Typically at least 8oz in volume, usually larger.

Latte art: the pattern or design created by pouring steamed milk on top of espresso. Only finely steamed milk is suitable for creating latte art. Popular patterns include the rosetta and heart.

Lever espresso machine: lever machines use manual force to drive a piston that generates the pressure required for espresso extraction. Common in the first half of the 20th century, but now largely superseded by electric pump-driven machines. Lever machines retain a small but passionate group of proponents.

Long black: a coffee beverage made by adding an espresso on top of hot water. Similar to an Americano, but usually shorter and the crema is preserved.

Macchiato: a coffee beverage consisting of espresso 'stained' with a dash of steamed milk (espresso macchiato) or a tall glass of steamed milk 'stained' with espresso (latte macchiato).

Macrofoam: stiff foam containing large

bubbles used to make a traditional cappuccino. Achieved by incorporating a greater quantity of air during the milk steaming process.

Microfoam: the preferred texture of finely-steamed milk for espresso-based coffee drinks. Essential for pouring latte art. Achieved by incorporating a lesser quantity of air during the milk steaming process.

Micro-lot coffee: coffee originating from a small, discrete area within a farm, typically benefiting from conditions favourable to the development of a particular set of characteristics. Micro-lot coffees tend to fetch higher prices due to their unique nature.

Mocha, caffè mocha: similar to a caffè latte, but with added chocolate syrup or powder.

Natural process: a simple method of processing coffee where whole cherries (with the bean inside) are dried on raised beds under the sun. Typically results in a lower acidity coffee with a heavier body and exotic flavours.

Over extracted: describes coffee with a bitter or burnt taste, resulting from ground coffee exposed to hot water for too long.

Peaberry: a small, round coffee bean formed when only one seed, rather than the usual two, develops in a coffee cherry. Peaberry beans produce a different flavour profile, typically lighter-bodied with higher acidy.

Piccolo: a short Italian coffee beverage made with espresso topped with an equal quantity of steamed milk. Traditionally served in a glass.

Pod: a self-contained, pre-ground, pre-pressed puck of coffee, individually wrapped inside a perforated paper filter. Mostly found in domestic espresso machines.

Often compatible only with certain equipment brands.

Pour over: a type of drip filter method in which a thin, steady stream of water is poured slowly over a bed of ground coffee contained within a filter cone.

Pouring kettle: a kettle with a narrow swan-neck spout specifically designed to deliver a steady, thin stream of water.

Portafilter: consists of a handle (usually plastic) attached to a metal cradle that holds the filter basket. Inserted into the group head and locked in place in preparation for making an espresso. Usually features a single or double spout on the underside to direct the flow of coffee into a cup.

Portafilter basket: a flat bottomed, bowl-shaped metal insert that sits in the portafilter and holds a bed of ground coffee. The basket has an array of tiny holes in the base allowing extracted coffee to seep through and pour into a cup.

Puck: immediately after an espresso extraction, the bed of spent coffee grounds forms compressed waste matter resembling a small hockey puck.

Pull: the act of pouring an espresso. The term originates from the first half of the 20th century when manual machines were the norm, and baristas pulled a lever to create an espresso.

Ristretto: a shorter 'restricted' shot of espresso. Made using the same dose and brew time as for a regular espresso, but with less water. The result is a richer and more intense beverage.

Roast: the process by which green coffee is heated in order to produce coffee beans ready for consumption. Caramelisation occurs as

Coffee Glossary contd.

intense heat converts starches in the bean to simple sugars, imbuing the bean with flavour and transforming its colour to a golden brown.

Robusta, Coffea canephora: the second most widely cultivated coffee species after arabica, robusta accounts for approximately 30% of the world's coffee. Robusta is hardier and grown at lower altitudes than arabica. It has a much higher caffeine content than arabica, and a less refined flavour. Commonly used in instant coffee blends.

Shot: a single unit of brewed espresso.

Single origin, single estate: coffee from one particular region or farm.

Siphon brewer, vacuum brewer: an unusual brewing method that relies on the action of a vacuum to draw hot water through coffee from one glass chamber to another. The resulting brew is remarkably clean.

Small batch: refers to roasting beans in small quantities, typically between 4-24kg, but sometimes larger.

Speciality coffee: a premium quality coffee scoring 80 points or above (from a total of 100) in the SCAA grading scale.

Steam wand: the protruding pipe found on an espresso machine that supplies hot steam used to froth and steam milk.

Stovetop, moka pot: a brewing method that makes strong coffee (but not espresso). Placed directly on a heat source, hot water is forced by steam pressure from the lower chamber to the upper chamber, passing through a bed of coffee.

Tamp: the process of distributing and pressing ground coffee into a compact bed

within the portafilter basket in preparation for brewing espresso. The degree of pressure applied during tamping is a key variable in espresso extraction. Too light and the brew water will percolate rapidly (tending to under extract), too firm and the water flow will be impeded (tending to over extract).

Tamper: the small pestle-like tool used to distribute and compact ground coffee in the filter basket.

Third wave coffee: the movement that treats coffee as an artisanal foodstuff rather than a commodity product. Quality coffee reflects its terroir, in a similar manner to wine.

Under extracted: describes coffee that has not been exposed to brew water for long enough. The resulting brew is often sour and thin-bodied.

V60: a popular type of pour over coffee brewer marketed by Hario. The product takes its name from the 60° angle of the V-shaped cone. Typically used to brew one or two cups only.

Washed process: one of the most common methods of processing coffee cherries. Involves fermentation in tanks of water to remove mucilage. Typically results in a clean and bright flavour profile with higher acidity.

Whole bean: coffee that has been roasted but not ground.

A-Z List of Coffee Venues

A-Z List of Coffee Venues contd.

UK COFFEE WEEK
APRIL 2014

WaterAid/Jake Lyell

A MASSIVE THANK YOU
TO ALL THE COFFEE SHOPS WHICH SUPPORTED UK COFFEE WEEK IN 2013

The money raised during this Week helped the Allegra Foundation to deliver Project Waterfall: bringing safe water, sanitation and hygiene to people in the remote community of the Mbulu District in Tanzania.

Thanks to Project Waterfall, over 8,000 people in this coffee-growing country now have access to safe water.

This is what one member of the community had to say...
"I was fetching water from 6km away so could not clean myself but now I have started bathing; our children were dirty now they are clean. Now we shall establish a kitchen garden and preparation of bricks so that we can shift from grass to brick made houses."

Many coffee shops which feature in this Guide played a key part in UK Coffee Week 2013, making this vital work possible. These included:

FOXCROFT AND GINGER
THE ATTENDANT
SALVATION JANE
LANTANA
LOOK MUM NO HANDS!
THE FLEET STREET PRESS
KAFFEINE
SHOREDITCH GRIND
TIMBERYARD
WHITE MULBERRIES
CLIMPSON & SONS
G&T

NUDE ESPRESSO
TAYLOR ST BARISTAS
OZONE COFFEE ROASTERS
MELROSE AND MORGAN
LEYAS
THE COFFEE WORKS PROJECT
MAISON D'ETRE COFFEE HOUSE
COFFEE CIRCUS
LOFT COFFEE COMPANY
WITH JAM AND BREAD
VOLCANO COFFEE WORKS
CRAFT COFFEE
ARTISAN
THE ETHIOPIAN COFFEE COMPANY

'PROJECT'
WATER
FALL
EVERYONE DESERVES CLEAN WATER

To find out more about **UK Coffee Week** and **Project Waterfall**, please visit www.ukcoffeeweek.com

Registered Charity Number: 1133541

THE LONDON COFFEE MAP

Notes, sketches, phone numbers etc.